0 011 962 98X 35

This book must be returned or ren

19 JUN 92 | 09. DEC | 12. 9 04. FEB 91

£1.20

92
94

THE MURDEROUS KIND

Max Haines' newspaper column is enjoyed by over two million readers in Canada each week. Here he provides fifty true tales of cons, thieves and murderers.

Also by Max Haines

BOTHERSOME BODIES

Max Haines

THE MURDEROUS KIND

Macdonald

A Macdonald Book

Copyright © 1983 by Max Haines

First published in Great Britain in 1989
by Macdonald & Co (Publishers) Ltd
London & Sydney

British Library Cataloguing in Publication Data

Haines, Max
    The murderous kind.
    1. Murder. Criminal investigation
    I. Title
    363.2'5

    ISBN 0 356 18155 3

Printed and bound in Great Britain by
Redwood Burn Limited, Trowbridge, Wiltshire

Macdonald & Co (Publishers) Ltd
Orbit House
1 New Fetter Lane
London EC4A 1AR

A member of Maxwell Macmillan Pergamon Publishing Corporation

CONTENTS

PART ONE
CONS AND SCAMS

THE PHONY PRINCE

Most of us have secret fantasies. Oh, to be a prince or princess, to have servants, be respected, honoured, and even loved by loyal subjects; to trade places with an honest to goodness member of a royal family for a year or even a month. It would be great fun. This is the story of a young charmer who pulled it off.

Harry Domela was born in Bauske, Russia in 1904. His middle-class parents spoke perfect German, and so did Harry. When World War I broke out his father and brothers were inducted into the Russian Army. They were never heard of again. When the front enveloped Bauske, Harry's mother simply disappeared. Ten-year-old Harry was placed in a children's home in Riga, where he remained until the war ended.

After the war, Harry gravitated to Berlin. Here the parentless, homeless teenager learned the tricks needed to stay alive. While leading the life of a vagrant, Harry managed to steal enough to survive. Ironically, it was only after he got a job at the Eden Hotel that he got into trouble. On his first day among the ranks of the gainfully employed, Harry swiped the hotel's silver cutlery. It's one thing to steal a bit of German sausage from a German butcher shop, but quite another to walk off with the Eden's silver spoons. Harry spent several uncomfortable months inconveniently detained in prison.

Upon his release he joined the hordes of social outcasts wandering the streets of German cities. Living by their wits Harry's companions included pimps, drunks, prostitutes, and bums. One day he met up with an unusual fellow bum. His companion was the down and out son of an old aristocratic German family. Harry was amazed that his friend had managed to retain his aristocratic air, his poise, and even his good manners.

Streetwise Harry recognized a good thing. His confident friend seemed to have no trouble obtaining a handout when he explained his temporary embarrassment to those more fortunate than himself. Sometimes the young man would even sweet talk a young fraülein into sharing his bed with him for an evening of high class fun and games. Harry watched his buddy in action and figured that he could be an aristocrat too.

Eventually Harry found employment as a door-to-door salesman selling cigars. He quickly found out that when he introduced himself as Harry Domela he had the unnerving experience of having doors slammed in his face. When he introduced himself as Count von Whatchamacallit he not only moved a few stogies, but sometimes the man of the house would press a few coins into his hand as well. When only the lady of the house was at home other more interesting objects were pressed upon Harry.

Still and all, there had to be something better in life than pushing cigars. Harry quit his job and moved on, making a precarious living posing as nobility of some sort or other. One day in Erfurt, Thuringia, he signed a hotel register Baron Korff. Harry was unceremoniously assigned a room on the fourth floor. Pulling the old aristocratic German family bit he requested a suite with a bath on the first floor. It didn't seem to work. No one was impressed.

Harry would show them a thing or two. He made a telephone call, in front of the hotel staff, to Prince Louis

Ferdinand, one of the old Kaiser's sons, who live in the Palace of Cecilienhof near Potsdam. Prince Louis wasn't at home, but the call had its effect. It happened that Harry bore a striking resemblance to His Imperial Royal Highness, Prince Wilhelm of Hohenzollern. The manager of the hotel couldn't take his eyes off Harry. Could he be lucky enough to have royalty staying at his hotel? Gott in Himmel, he shouted, and dashed off to his office to study a group photo of the Royal Family. Sure as strudel, his guest, using the phony name of Baron Korff, was in reality Prince Wilhelm.

Harry Domela never dreamt he would fall into this one. Despite his insistence that he was Baron Korff, the hotel staff was instructed to refer to him only as Your Highness. Harry wasn't allowed to lift a finger. Everyone bowed and scraped in his presence. His every wish was catered to. Our boy never had it so good.

Still, Harry was no fool. He knew that sooner or later he would be exposed. The reluctant imposter moved to Berlin and again checked into a hotel as Baron Korff. He was greeted with a knowing wink. Harry couldn't believe it. His phony reputation had preceded him. Everyone was in on the secret. Prince Wilhelm was moving about Germany as Baron Korff. Harry lived it up for a week or so and then made up his mind. If the citizenry insisted on making him a prince, then let them. He returned to Erfurt with the express intention of living like a prince.

The Erfurt hotel manager thought he must be the most fortunate man in all Germany to once again have His Highness as a guest. The Mayor of Erfurt paid his respects. This time Harry signed Prince Wilhelm in the golden book of the town. His Highness was in great demand and travelled extensively throughout Thuringia, opening fairs and bazaars. Harry loved to have the train stop at every town and deliver a little speech to the locals before pulling out of the station to their applause.

Harry became a fair to middling after-dinner speaker at charity banquets. He never failed to sell out the house. Still, he knew that sooner or later it must all come to an end. To prolong his princely life Harry would confidentially call on the highest ranking army official in every town. He would introduce himself as Prince Wilhelm and request that the officer assist him in suppressing all newspaper accounts of his visit to the town. The officers always cooperated in suppressing the newspaper stories, but Harry knew that they couldn't do a thing about rumours. In this way he kept his face out of the papers and continued to receive the royal treatment.

Harry pulled off his ruse for months. In January 1927 the bubble burst. A suspicious hotel manager decided to check. It took only a telephone call to Potsdam to verify that the real Prince Wilhelm had not been to Thuringia for several months.

Harry headed hastily for Berlin. When he arrived there his exploits were front-page news in every paper in the country. Posing as a derelict, Harry tried to join the French Foreign Legion. He was spotted by plainclothes detectives, who unceremoniously placed him in a Cologne jail.

Harry's little charade had a strange effect on the German public. Everyone enjoyed the prank. No real harm had been done and the populace had had a good belly laugh. A German newspaper instituted a Domela fund to help finance Harry's defence.

While awaiting trial, a publisher offered Harry an advance of 25,000 marks, then over $5,000, for his memoirs. Harry, who obviously had a series of hidden talents, wrote his autobiography. It was an immediate success, and sold over 70,000 copies as soon as it was released.

Harry was so popular at his trial that all the witnesses he had duped swore that they had gained by his deception rather than suffered from it. He was found guilty and received a prison term of seven months, the exact time he had already spent in custody. He walked out of court a free man.

Harry was now a national hero. He even had the gall to visit the authentic Prince Wilhelm's mother, Her Imperial Highness, the Crown Princess Cecile. Harry stayed for tea.

Later Her Highness stated that he was a charming guest and kept her amused by telling stories of how he had posed as her son.

Harry's book continued to sell for three years. In 1930 a movie, *The False Prince*, was made about his exploits. It starred none other than Harry Domela.

As war clouds appeared over Germany, Harry left the country and has never been heard of since.

THÉRÈSE'S MYSTERIOUS TRUNK

The weird and wonderful world of the genuine con artist attracts those ladies and gentlemen who have been blessed with nerves of steel. How else could a former stockbroker con the good citizens of Arizona out of half of their state? How else could a scalliwagg, posing as a count, sell the Eiffel Tower, not once, but twice?

Some artists train themselves for half a lifetime in preparation for the one big confidence game. The sting is firmly planted, the loot gathered up, and the mark is left holding the bag. Other practitioners of the devious art enter the world of con more gradually.

Madam Thérèse Humbert had no intention of becoming one of the most refined and successful confidence ladies who ever lived. It just happened. You see, Thérèse's papa was sort of the village bum. The Aurignac family lived in Bauzelles, near Toulouse, France, in what we could call abject poverty. Besides Thérèse and Papa, there was a school-age sister, Marie, and two brothers, Romain and Emile.

Now, Papa wasn't an ordinary run of the mill bum. He always maintained a certain dignity and aristocratic bearing, even when he was in his cups, which was often. Papa would ramble on incessantly about his noble birth, insisting to everyone who would listen that in reality he was a count. The old man was usually tossed a few coins to keep him quiet. While the payment for them was not enough to make him rich, his tall tales served to keep him well oiled all day and most nights, while his two sons worked in the fields, and Thérèse kept his home spick-and-span.

No one remembers whether Papa became senile and actually believed his own wild stories or if he just became cunning in his declining years. The wily old gent went into an antique shop in Toulouse and purchased a decrepit oak chest, which he outfitted with impressive seals and locks. He then revealed to his cronies that the chest held the deed to a huge château, which would be passed along to his children when he died. The story brought Papa a few drinks, but little else. In Jan. 1874 the old man died. The impressive locked trunk was opened and found to contain nothing but one solid, lonesome, ordinary brick.

In order to keep the family together Thérèse got a job as a laundry maid for M. Gustave Humbert, the mayor of Toulouse. The mayor had a son Frederick, who was studying law at the University of Toulouse. On warm summer evenings Fred would tear himself away from his law books and devote himself to the study of Thérèse. To keep Fred's innermost fires burning, our Thérèse let it slip that it was true that she and her family would eventually inherit the Château de Marcotte. It was just a matter of time. Thérèse's two brothers helped perpetuate the rumour. Before long, most people believed that the Aurignac family would someday inherit a fortune. Fred was so enraptured with Thérèse's physical charms, as well as her potential wealth, that he asked her to marry him. Mayor Humbert, who had moved to Paris to further his political career, almost blew a gasket. His son and the laundry maid! He wouldn't hear of it.

Despite M. Humbert's objections, Thérèse and Fred became man and wife. In the meantime the former mayor struck paydirt when he was appointed Minister of Justice of France.

Fred managed to eke out a living at his law practice. Many

nights, he would inquire about his wife's future inheritance. Thérèse became increasingly evasive and adept at changing the subject. She never complained of having a headache.

Thérèse and Fred moved to Paris. In March 1881, Thérèse hatched the scheme that was to make her one of the world's most successful con artists. The scheme was so fantastic, so incredible, that it was believed by everyone. The phony story spread by word of mouth from one aristocrat to another.

It seems Thérèse Humbert, daughter-in-law of the Minister of Justice, had had a great adventure. She had boarded a train at Grenelle bound for Bel Air. At about the halfway point in her journey she heard a loud groan coming from the adjoining compartment. Disregarding any danger, she unhesitatingly left her own compartment and entered the neighbouring one. Thérèse found an elderly gentleman in some distress. He had possibly suffered a heart attack. Thérèse loosened his collar and administered smelling salts. The elderly gent came around, was most appreciative and, before parting, took Thérèse's address.

Two years passed. Thérèse was informed by American lawyers that the elderly gentleman was Robert Henry Crawford, a Chicago millionaire, who had died, leaving £4 million. Crawford's entire estate was to be divided among his American nephews, Robert and Henry, and Thérèse and her younger sister, Marie. Thérèse explained that she vaguely remembered mentioning her sister to Crawford. Anyway, who was she to question the idiosyncrasies of the very wealthy?

When questioned by friends, Thérèse declared that her lawyers had been in touch with the American lawyers representing the Crawford nephews. The two Crawfords were millionaires in their own right. Everything was legitimate and amicable. A long distance friendship had developed between the two brothers and Thérèse and Marie. During the course of corresponding with the Crawfords, a photo of Marie was sent to them. Later the Crawfords' lawyers strongly recommended that one of the brothers marry Marie when she finished school. While this may seem somewhat far fetched today we must remember that the very rich have a penchant for keeping their wealth in the family.

The deal was cooked. Legal documents were signed. The bonds and securities representing the inheritance were turned over to Thérèse, together with a court order stipulating that they be kept in a sealed safe.

Looking back, it's kind of hard to swallow, but at the time, the story was accepted without question. The two sisters began to live like millionaires. Bankers scurried to lend them huge sums against the day the safe would be opened. Everyone would be paid off, and presumably everyone would live happily ever after. Romain and Emile (remember them, Thérèse's brothers) managed to get into the act. They moved into luxurious quarters in Paris. Thérèse, always one with a flair for the dramatic, installed a sealed, ribbon-bedecked safe in her brothers' apartments, for all to see.

Thérèse and Fred were sought-after guests at every great ball and social event in France. They lived like royalty, in elegant châteaus. Thérèse knew that the con needed to be fed to stay alive. This she did over the years in ingenious ways. Once she orchestrated a visit by one of the fictional Crawfords to Paris. Thérèse paid the actor well. From time to time Thérèse would create some news to add credibility to the con. She arranged to have the Crawford brothers sue her. In all the legal battles concerning the inheritance, Thérèse footed the bills for both the plaintiff and the defence. In the meantime she and her entire family lived high off the hog. To satisfy the few financiers who insisted on being paid, Thérèse merely borrowed from someone else to pay off the current debt.

As years passed, the need to raise money became more acute. Thérèse decided to go into the investment business. Together with her brothers she opened a firm that she called Rente Viagère, an investment house where small amounts could be invested at high interest rates. Business flourished. The suckers were paid off in other investors' money, and so the game went merrily along.

Thérèse's wine bill exceeded the equivalent of £100 per month. Her florist bill was over £500. The end came in 1901, when several businesses went bankrupt, claiming it was Thérèse's fault for not repaying their loans. Even these men didn't realize there was a fraud in progress. They thought that Thérèse had used up all of her share of the £4 million in the celebrated safe.

Thérèse's creditors were successful in obtaining a court order allowing the safe to be opened. The ceremony was to take place on May 9, 1902. The night before, Thérèse, her sister Marie, and her two brothers hastily left Paris. The safe was duly opened. It contained one solitary brick. Wherever he was, Papa Aurignac must have had a chuckle. The same scheme had netted him only a few drinks. His daughter had milked millions from it and had lived like a queen for over twenty years.

The law caught up with Thérèse and her family in Madrid, Spain. Marie was let off the hook, but Thérèse and her two brothers stood trial at the Assize Court of the Seine. Thérèse received four years solitary confinement. Romain was put away for three years, while Emile was sentenced to only two years in prison.

At the conclusion of her trial reporters asked Thérèse if it had all been worth it. Indignantly she replied, "Of course not. You see, there really is another trunk containing...'."

ROB PETER TO
PAY PAUL

Carlo Ponzi sat on the steps of his tenement house in Boston and watched the suckers returning home from work. There had to be a way to relieve them of their hard-earned dollars. Day after day he sat and thought and then one day he came up with a scheme so simple it boggles the imagination.

"Hey Giuseppe, come here. If you lend me ten dollars, I'll pay you back fifteen dollars in forty-five days. I'll meet you right here on the steps and pay you fifty percent interest." Giuseppe decided to take a chance. The next day Carlo again sat on his step. "Hey Luigi come here. If you lend me ten dollars, I'll pay you back fifteen dollars in forty-five days." Luigi fell for it. Forty-five days passed and sure enough, Carlo met Giuseppe and offered him the fifteen dollars. Giuseppe said, "What the hell, keep it and give me another fifty percent interest for forty-five days."

So it started, the rob Peter to pay Paul scheme that was to rock the financial establishments of the United States.

Carlo had immigrated to America from Italy as a seventeen-year-old. He started off his career as a dishwasher and then as a waiter in New York. He drifted to Montreal and rose from waiting on tables to swindling Italian immigrants. He ran a service that assured immigrants of sending money home to Italy in a safe and efficient manner. Unfortunately for the trusting newcomers, most of their hard-earned cash found its way into Carlo's pockets. The police in their annoying way managed to stick a forgery wrap on our hero and he ended up doing three years in prison. Once out of prison he took to smuggling Italians across the Canadian border to the U.S. Carlo was sent away for three more years to contemplate the error of his ways.

Carlo decided to try his luck in Boston. Here he met, wooed, and wed Rose Guecco, whose father owned a wholesale grocery business. It didn't take Ponzi long before he had the business bankrupt. He then took a job as a $16-a-week clerk.

The year was 1918. The war in Europe was over and the good times that were to last through the Roaring Twenties, had just begun. Wages were on the rise. People had more money than ever before. Wage earners were looking for a place to invest small amounts of savings.

Along came Ponzi.

There were enough Giuseppes and Luigis around that soon he opened Ponzi's Securities Exchange Company at 27 School St. in Boston. The money poured in at such a rate that even Ponzi couldn't believe it. He had to come up with some explanation of how he could pay fifty percent interest in forty-five days. He claimed to have agents in Europe buying depreciated European money, converting the currency into international postal coupons, which when sent to the U.S. were redeemable at face value into American dollars. To hear Ponzi tell it, Rockefeller and all the banking wizards in the U.S. were doing it. The only difference was that they were keeping tremendous profits to themselves. He was sharing the wealth.

The money continued to pour in at the rate of tens of thousands of dollars a day. Carlo in the worst of times was a natty dresser, but now he was a real fashion plate. He arrived at the office each morning in his chauffeur-driven limousine. Usually the crowd pushing to invest their money had to make a path so he could get into his office. Carlo was canny enough to have a lot of money on display. There were the crowded deposit wickets and the deserted withdrawal wickets. Ponzi became so prosperous that he bought a substantial interest in two legitimate firms, the Hanover Trust Company and J.P. Poole Co. He also bought Rose a mansion.

Probably the single biggest contributor to Ponzi's downfall was the fact that he was too successful. The federal government started to look into his affairs. They checked with the postal authorities, who assured them that his scheme was impractical and told everyone who would listen that such large amounts of postal coupons were never purchased by Ponzi's Company. Foreign governments made statements to the effect that a dollar's worth of coupons would cost an American dollar.

It was one thing to point out his method of making money was obviously false and quite another to prove that any law had been broken. Ponzi continued on until July 1920, when the U.S. government decided to do an official audit on him. When the news became widespread, there was something of a run on his establishment. Ponzi paid each withdrawal on demand plus any interest due. It seemed that he had an inexhaustible supply of cash. Even the auditors couldn't find anything wrong. He had complete records of cash receipts and disbursements. What he didn't show was the source of his profits. He simply refused, saying it was his secret. The government placed a restraining order on the company, not allowing it to accept deposits while the investigation was going on. The withdrawals started to dwindle.

Ponzi hired one William McMaster to shore up his public relations. McMaster issued the statement that Ponzi had never completed a foreign financial transaction of any kind. This started another run. Again Ponzi paid off in full to every person who wanted their money. Not only did he give them back their money but he also served coffee and hot dogs to everyone who came into the office.

He kept up the charade as long as he could, but in the end the cash ran out. On August 9, 1920, his bank issued a statement that it wouldn't honour Ponzi's cheques. On August 11, his former police record was made public. This was the final straw. People demanded their money. Ponzi actually feared for his life and he demanded and got police protection. During the proceedings that followed, all assets, including Rose's mansion, furniture, and her three cars, were seized by the courts.

Later, auditors placed the total take at fifteen million dollars, of which three-quarters was paid back to creditors. At one time Ponzi had had over forty thousand individual investors on the hook.

How did he expect to keep on paying out more than he took in? No one knows for sure, but he may have figured one big financial killing would recoup enough to make up the huge deficit.

On October 21, 1920, the now penniless Ponzi received five years' imprisonment for embezzlement. He was released in 1924 and stood trial on further charges. The following year he received an additional nine years. When he was released from prison in 1934, he was deported to Italy. He offered his financial wizardry to Mussolini and was hired, but the dictator soon found out that Ponzi wasn't a financial genius, and dismissed him. Finally Carlo got work with an Italian airline and was transferred to Rio de Janeiro. The airline promptly folded.

Ponzi, poverty stricken, with poor eyesight, and partially paralyzed, died in a charity ward in Brazil in 1949.

THE FIX WAS IN

The not so lily-white sport of college basketball became positively soiled in 1951 when it was discovered that the cream of American youth were not giving their all for dear old Alma Mater. The fact is, some of the elongated boys were more interested in lining their pockets than filling baskets. Fixing the results of college basketball games was so widespread in 1950 that the practice was common knowledge.

One of the culprits behind the shenanigans taking place on the basketball courts was Salvatore Sollazzo. Sal was a quiet Italian boy who was born on New Year's Eve, 1904, in Palermo, Sicily. His family immigrated to the United States when Sal was only fifteen months old. His papa was a jewellery maker and repairman back in Italy and continued in his trade in his new home of Brooklyn, New York.

Sal attended public school and got average grades. After school he worked in his father's jewellery store. When his father died, Sal took over the family business. A year later, in 1931, the jewellery store went bankrupt.

Like all hard-working, clean living young men who wish to surmount adversity, Sal started out again at the bottom of the heap. He peddled jewellery door to door. The good citizens of Brooklyn did not climb over each other to patronize the chubby, balding peddler who knocked at their doors. Times were tough. Sal decided to take a chance. He obtained a temporary position as lookout for a group of men who planned on entering the jewellery industry the easy way. They robbed a jewellery wholesaler on West 31st St.

Sal drew a rather harsh seven and a half to fifteen years as a guest of the state of New York. He spent the next five years at that well-known resort for chaps who insist on absconding with other people's belongings – Sing Sing.

After being released from prison, Sal secured a position as a jewellery salesman, drawing the princely sum of fifteen dollars a week. He worked hard, bettered himself by changing jobs and, above all, saved almost every cent he made. By 1940 he went into business for himself, manufacturing wedding and birthstone rings under the name Francine Mfg. Jewellers Inc.

For three years Sal struggled along. Then, a quirk of fate allowed him to make a killing. Platinum was declared a scarce war material, and Sal had been shrewd enough to stockpile the metal. When the price of platinum doubled overnight, he made a quick $50,000 on the black market.

With this windfall Sal expanded his business and, by 1944, was the fourth largest wedding ring company in the United States, with over a hundred employees. The money poured in. Unfortunately Sal discovered that the Bureau of Internal Revenue had the distressing habit of insisting on an extremely large cut of his profits. To circumvent the income tax boys, Sal pursuaded several large customers to make their cheques out to names other than Francine Mfg. These cheques were then cashed by Sal and the proceeds smartly put into his pocket for safekeeping. They were conveniently never reported as income on Francine's books.

Everything was coming up roses. Sal usually travelled with a pair of mink-clad beauties, one on each arm. He frequented all the better watering holes, and had a box seat at Yankee Stadium. To round out his new-found interest in the sporting life, Sal loved to sip a cool one at Belmont or Aqueduct Racetracks and watch the nags dash by.

Sal began to bet heavily. Gambling became an all-consuming passion. Some days he would have $5,000 on a baseball game and another $5,000 on a fight at the Gardens, all this after losing up to ten big ones at Aqueduct on the same day. Sal could and did drop $20,000 on bad days.

Despite an excellent income from his jewellery business, Sal went into debt to feed his bigtime gambling habit. To alleviate the constant demands for money, he took to dealing with gold smugglers. Because he was in the wedding ring business, Sal had access to gold at the government-pegged price of $35 per troy ounce. He merely made it available to the smugglers at a tidy little profit. Later, it was ascertained that he cleared $2,500 per week by illegal trafficking in gold.

His extravagant gambling habits continued. The hungry monster was now grinding up all the profits from his business plus the income from his illegal activities. There had to be some way out. That's when Sal met what appeared to be the answer to all his problems.

Eddie Gard was a basketball player for Long Island University. Sal and Eddie met in a nightclub in Oct. 1949. Before we delve into the world of college basketball, it would be useful to explain basketball's betting procedures. All bets placed on basketball games are even money. The odds are calculated by the point spread. For instance, if you bet on Team A to defeat Team B by ten points, and they win the game by only nine points, you lose. As the fat girl said to the thin girl, the spread is everything.

Eddie and two of his teammates agreed to cooperate with our boy Sal. The three athletes each received $100 in advance as a sort of goodwill gesture. They were to receive a further $1,000 each per game when the fix was in.

On Jan. 17, the three athletes, Gard, Adolph Bijos, and Dick Feurtado were to play against North Carolina State. Long Island University was favoured to win by a wide margin. Sal bet $6,000 on North Carolina State. The three players played so poorly that L.I.U. lost the game 55 to 52. Sal paid out $3,000 to the players and was left with $3,000 profit. Not bad for one night's work.

There was one little incident, which Gard reported to Sal. The star of the team, Sherman White, had berated Gard, Bijos, and Feurtado in the locker room after the game. In essence, Mr. White expressed the opinion that his three team-mates stunk out the joint. Sal invited White to join the party. It wasn't difficult. Sherm thought the invitation was the greatest thing since Santa Claus.

Two more games remained on L.I.U.'s schedule that season. In February L.I.U. lost 83 to 65 to the University of Cincinnati, and in March they were downed by Syracuse University 80 to 52. Sal collected on both games.

During the summer Mr. Gard, who was ineligible to play the following season, stayed in close contact with Sal. Eddie had become Sal's unofficial assistant in charge of the big fix.

Eddie advised Sal that the fix was in for the upcoming game between L.I.U. and Kansas State. L.I.U. were six-point favourites. In Dec. 1950 they squeaked out a 60 to 59 win. Sal collected $7,500.

Gard, who was an ambitious young man, informed Sal that he now had two players, Ed Warner and Floyd Lane, who played for City College of New York, in his stable. This time, with C.C.N.Y. scheduled to play Brigham Young, Sal wanted the players to exceed the point spread. What Sal couldn't know was that two other players on the C.C.N.Y. team had been bought off by other gamblers. It was quite a basketball game. One half the team was trying their hardest to pull off an outstanding victory, while the other half missed every shot. C.C.N.Y. lost the game, and Sal dropped $5,000.

Sal contacted the two players who were in the employ of another gambler and offered them more money. They agreed. Sal now had most of the C.C.N.Y. team in his pocket. When C.C.N.Y., a fourteen-point favourite, lost by seventeen points to Missouri, some eyebrows were raised. Broadway bookies were becoming leery of accepting Sal's bets on either L.I.U. or C.C.N.Y. To make matters worse, the teams were suspect. Sal was also hearing rumblings from other directions.

The Internal Revenue boys couldn't understand the low

sales figures on Francine Mfg.'s books when the company's gold purchases were so high.

The basketball really hit the foul line when L.I.U.'s coach received an anonymous letter accusing Bigos and White of fixing games. When accused by their coach the players denied any knowledge of a fix, but the experience scared the daylights out of them. They decided to retire from the fixing business then and there. Inconsiderate lads that they were, they didn't bother to tell Sal. He placed as much money as he could in the next game, betting Duquesne to win over L.I.U. He almost had a fit as he watched his boys play with stout-hearted determination and ran up an 84 to 52 win.

The Duquesne loss was the beginning of the end for Sal. Because of an unrelated fixed game, many players, including Sal's entire stable, had their phones tapped. Soon District Attorney Frank Hogan had enough evidence to arrest several players. Sal was arrested as well, but this wasn't his only problem.

One of his gold smugglers was apprehended and, to save his skin, revealed where he had purchased the gold. At the same time, the tax people closed in on Sal. They filed a whopping tax lien of over a million dollars against him.

In the end the wayward players received penalties ranging from suspended sentences to three years in prison. Sal received a sentence of from eight to sixteen years on the basketball charges, two years for gold smuggling, and one year each on five counts of tax evasion. Sal's legitimate business, Francine Mfg., went down the pipe to pay back taxes.

As the prison doors closed behind him, Sal still owed $12,000 in fines and over a million dollars in back taxes.

SALAD OIL, ANYONE?

It is one thing to procure a gun and rob a bank of a few thousand dollars. Any clown can give it a try. But it is another thing to grab a financial institution for several million dollars. That takes the combined machinations of a gentleman and a scholar. Anthony DeAngelis tried to be both.

Born in 1915 to poor Italian immigrants, Tino lived in a walk-up cold water tenement in the Bronx, New York City. Tino had a brother and two sisters. Times were tough.

As Tino grew to manhood he displayed the sterling characteristics of hard work and honesty, which led his parents to feel that they had raised a future man of the cloth. Tino obviously had other ideas. He was to become the greatest swindler ever to come out of the good old U.S. of A.

Tino quit high school at sixteen to enter the world of commerce. He became a clerk in a large fish and meat market. Within three years he was manager of the place, which employed two hundred workers. Not bad for a lad of twenty. Ambition forced Tino to seek greener pastures. He left his managerial post at the market for a foreman's position at the City Provision Co., a hog processing organization. It was while processing pork that Tino met the future Mrs. DeAngelis. Virginia Bracconeri became infatuated with short, fat, but charming Tino. Within a year the pair were married, and a year after that the union was blessed with a son, Thomas.

In 1938, with his savings of $2,000, Tino opened his own business, the M and D Hog Cutters. His first year in business brought a net profit of $100,000. The successful operation was soon processing 3,000 hogs a day and turning a tidy $300,000 profit each year. Tino was a big man in pork. His largest customer was the U.S. Army.

Now a millionaire, Tino decided to expand his horizons. In 1949 he purchased the Adolph Gobel Co. of North Bergen, N.J., a well-known meat packing firm listed on the American Stock Exchange. Tino received a contract from the U.S. Agricultural Dept. to supply 18 million pounds of smoked meat to be distributed throughout the country for school children's lunches. The first deliveries didn't pass government standards and Gobel was cut off as a supplier. There was also an incident whereby the government accused Gobel of bumping up the weights of the delivered product. It was all too much; in 1953 the company was placed in bankruptcy by creditors, but allowed to operate under supervision in an attempt to bail itself out. President Tino was ousted.

In 1955 Tino left the meat packing business and plunged headlong into salad oil. He recognized an opportunity when he saw one. The U.S. had embarked on a huge Food for Peace program. Here's how it worked. Certain products overproduced in the U.S. were eligible for the program. They were to be shipped to underdeveloped countries. Private companies would ship to the hungry countries, but the bill would be picked up by Uncle Sam. In 1955 there was a surplus of salad oil in the U.S.

Our boy Tino organized the Allied Crude Vegetable Oil Refining Corp. with the help of twenty-two former colleagues at Gobel and a half a million dollars. He set up business in a rundown building in Bayonne, N.J., amidst a sea of old petroleum storage tanks. Tino went to work installing a refinery to convert crude vegetable oil into salad oil. He also instituted a program to clean up the petroleum tanks for use in storing the salad oil.

Business boomed right from the start. Tino offered the export companies a good deal. He bought crude oil in the mid west, transported it to his refinery by rail, refined the product, and presented salad oil ready for overseas markets to the large export companies. Tino provided all these services cheaper than any of his competitors.

There was one small catch, and that was the large amount of cash needed to purchase, transport, and refine the oil. The large export companies loaned Allied hundreds of thousands of dollars in order for Tino to implement his scheme. The fat little man was pulling it off. Everyone was making money, although it was difficult to understand how Allied was actually turning a profit. Two large export companies, Continental Grain and Bunge Corp. were Tino's largest customers.

By 1958 Allied and its several subsidiaries had annual sales of over $200 million. Little by little Allied's competitors fell by the wayside. Tino's empire was exporting 75 percent of all edible oils being shipped out of the U.S. Allied, who always paid the highest prices for the product, had become the biggest purchaser of vegetable oils in the country.

Tino himself worked sixteen hours a day. To drum up business he cooked deals in Rome, Madrid, Amsterdam, and other world capitals. Huge contracts for salad oil were awarded to Allied through the export companies. Tino DeAngelis, who quit school at sixteen, was now king.

Tino neither drank nor smoked. He did have one little diversion. Her name was Lillian Pascarelli, a forty-year-old lady who helped him ease the tensions of a busy day at the office. Lillian was rewarded for her assistance with little trinkets, like a $10,000 platinum necklace and a $9,000 diamond ring. Lillian was also one of those fortunate women who sported both a mink and sable coat. On rainy days she drove her Chevy, ostensibly to keep the Caddy high and dry in the garage of her $65,000 home. Not bad work if you can get it. Life went on in this pleasant way until Tino became exceedingly greedy.

*   *   *

Just about everyone at some time or other has used American Express travellers' cheques. Throughout the world millions carry American Express credit cards. The huge multi-million dollar organization is above reproach. The very essence of the organization is based on explicit trust and faith in its integrity.

The public is unaware that American Express is involved in many enterprises. In 1944, through a subsidiary, American Express Field Warehousing Corp., it entered the warehousing business. At the time it seemed like a natural and progressive step. All American Express had to do was take over the supervision of customers' warehouses, guaranteeing that what was supposed to be in storage at the warehouse was in fact there. They could then issue warehouse receipts to the customers, who in turn could present the receipts to their bank as collateral for loans. Naturally, only warehouse receipts of large trusted organizations were honoured by banks. American Express Warehousing fell into this category. Despite their impeccable reputation, the warehousing end of American Express' operation did not flourish. In fact, it lost money for several years.

Tino DeAngelis called on the president of American Express Warehousing, Donald K. Miller. Miller was given a guided tour of Tino's tank farm at Bayonne and was greatly impressed with the modern stainless steel refining plant. Within a week Miller had made up his mind to do business with Allied. There was one technicality, however. DeAngelis was a former bankrupt. Tino himself came up with the solution to circumvent this problem. American Express would take over supervision of Allied's inventory. They would issue warehouse receipts to Allied, who would turn them over to the large export companies, who in turn would put them up at their bank for collateral. In this way Allied would get paid for their inventory immediately. American Express would of course receive fat commissions on all transactions.

American Express Warehousing approved the deal, the

large export companies approved the deal, and the largest banks in the U.S. approved the deal. Anthony DeAngelis was now in the position he wanted.

As far as Tino was concerned American Express Warehouse receipts were the same as cash. All he had to do was present them and receive a cheque. Of course, in theory, the salad oil represented by the receipts had to be in storage tanks at Bayonne. These tanks were inspected periodically by American Express officials. What no one knew except Tino and his boys was that several tanks had been rigged. A small compartment extending from the top of the tank to the bottom was always chock full of oil. Tino's employees always led the American Express officials to do their soundings in this compartment. The balance of these tanks were filled with salt water.

Besides this subterfuge, Tino had installed a complex system of pipes, allowing legitimate oil to be moved from tank to tank before American Express officials checked them.

In short, American Express was certifying millions of pounds of oil that didn't exist. The amount of money turned over to DeAngelis for the phantom oil was staggering. Once started, Tino couldn't stop, because with every deal he was losing money. His swindle required nourishment, like an addict. During 1962 DeAngelis converted $320 million of warehouse receipts into cash. At any given time over $50 million was for non-existent oil.

Allied became the number one exporter of salad oil in the U.S. In fact, at one point Allied's records showed an inventory of more salad oil in Bayonne than existed in the entire country. No one noticed.

Tino was living like the millionaire he had become, but he had one gnawing fear. While he had enough actual oil for normal business operations he could not fill an extraordinarily large order. His fictional oil was rapidly becoming most of his inventory.

That's when Tino came up with the scheme that would prove to be his downfall. Prospects for demand for oil from foreign countries was high in 1963. Tino decided to buy on margin all the future contracts for salad oil that were offered for sale. In simple terms, he could buy a contract that obligated him to deliver oil at a future date for very little money down. If the price rose he could deliver the oil at a substantial profit, or merely sell the contract at the same profit. If the price dropped, Tino had to come up with the increased margin requirement within twenty-four hours. Each day he madly purchased future contracts for salad oil so that the price wouldn't fall. The magnitude of his scheme was astronomical. Within a short time Allied had 22,600 contracts worth $160 million, for which it had paid very little money. If the price of salad oil dropped as much as one cent a pound, Allied would have to pay $13,560,000 within twenty-four hours. It was a dangerous game.

Commodity brokers became apprehensive and limited Allied's credit. When Tino attempted to switch brokers, the Commodity Exchange decided to investigate Allied. The game was over.

When the smoke cleared the total of Tino's fraud approached $200 million. Banks, brokers, and businessmen were all caught holding the bag. Several never recovered and were forced into bankruptcy. Chase-Manhattan bit the bullet for approximately $30 million. American Express, with its reputation at stake, is believed to have made good on $60 million of phony warehouse receipts.

Months later, when Tino finally faced the music in court, he pleaded guilty to three charges of circulating forged warehouse receipts and one charge of conspiracy. He received a sentence of ten years in prison.

If you don't recall hearing about the greatest single swindle in U.S. history, there is a reason. The case broke on Nov. 22, 1963, the day John F. Kennedy was assassinated.

PART TWO
RELATIVES

ASSORTED WIVES

Throughout the checkered history of crime we often come across gentlemen who favour having more than one wife at a time. Some insist on having two. Then there are those rare birds who positively cannot do without several. Some of these gentlemen have the temperament and indeed the capacity to love all their wives dearly. But, alas, there are those rascals who just don't give a damn one way or the other.

Arthur Goslett was a rascal. Using the name Capt. Arthur Godfrey (no connection whatever with the late television personality of the same name) he operated during the First World War in England. Resplendent in the glamorous uniform of a naval officer, the captain carried himself with that arrogant air so common to con artists and bigamists. Despite the uniform, the captain left a lot to be desired in the looks department. His face was marked by a constant scowl, which gave him a mean appearance. This, coupled with a pair of eyes that appeared too small for the rest of his face, produced a sinister impression. But Casanova was not known for his looks either.

By 1918 the dashing captain had gone through so many marriages that, later on, investigating officers gave up counting. It is only necessary for us to realize that, despite all his marriages, Arthur had a bona fide wife alive and well and living in Armitage Mansions, Golders Green, London.

Mrs. Goslett wasn't exactly ignorant of her husband's

activities. Some time earlier she had discovered one of Arthur's bigamous alliances and had seen to it that he was thrown into jail for his indiscretion. Arthur had learned his lesson and was now a dutiful husband, or so Mrs. Goslett thought. In fact, the brief jail term only served to revitalize Arthur's amorous tendencies.

In 1918 a lady named Daisy Holt ventured upon the scene. That is to say, she bumped into the captain one day on the street. Apologetic, pleasant, and charming, the captain insisted on accompanying her to her sparsely furnished room. In a few months Daisy, with a decided degree of apprehension, advised the captain, whom she believed to be single, that she was pregnant. Daisy requested one thing and one thing only. Would the dear captain marry her and live happily ever after? Poor Daisy didn't know it, but she was speaking to one of the most married men of all time. Arthur consented without a whimper. What was one marriage more or less, anyway? The phony ceremony was performed in Feb. 1919.

Captain and Mrs. Godfrey took a flat in the Kew District of London. But, alas, the condition of pregnancy did not agree with Daisy. She became so ill she had to spend some time in a nursing home before giving birth to a boy.

Upon being discharged from the nursing home Daisy was chagrined to discover that the captain had given up their flat. There she was, barefoot and no longer pregnant, with no place to live. When faced with this embarrassing situation the captain confessed that his real name was Goslett, not Godfrey, and that there was a Mrs. Goslett and three tiny Gosletts.

The captain had a great idea. Why shouldn't Daisy and the new addition move in with Mrs. Goslett and the three children? It would be simple. Arthur's wife had never met his brother Percy or Percy's wife. Percy had recently died. Daisy could pose as Percy's wife and all six could live happily under one roof.

At first Daisy would have nothing to do with such a wild

scheme, but the captain was quick to point out that she didn't have many options. Daisy decided to give it a whirl. Dressed in mourning black, she was accepted by Mrs. Goslett without question.

Daisy at this time refused to have intercourse with the captain, and securely fastened her bedroom door each evening. This annoyed the captain, but things could be worse. For one thing, Mrs. Goslett and Daisy got along famously. In fact, Mrs. Goslett became decidedly fond of her kind, helpful sister-in-law.

Then one day, an old acquaintance recognized Daisy on the street as Captain Godfrey's wife. When she heard her addressed as Mrs. Percy Goslett she smelled a rat. Busybody that she was, she called on the Captain's wife and informed her of her suspicions. Mrs. Goslett's reaction was a surprise. She was sympathetic to the plight of Daisy and her baby, but insisted that Daisy find a room elsewhere.

The Captain was furious. Now that the truth was known, what would be so terrible if the present arrangements were to continue? You can say what you will about Captain Arthur, but he did have gall. Of course, Mrs. Goslett had the upper hand, for she could always holler bigamy and have Arthur tossed into jail. Besides, Arthur had a bit of a secret. Throwing caution to the wind, he had gone out and acquired a third wife.

He promised his first wife that he would spend some time looking for suitable quarters for Daisy and her baby. Although most of Arthur's waking moments and, we can only assume, some of his sleeping ones as well, were spent on affairs sexual, his mind now turned to murder. It was obvious that his one legitimate wife was spoiling all his fun. Mrs. Goslett had to go.

On the pretense of looking at a new home, Arthur and his wife headed for Hendon at 9:30 on the evening of May 1, 1920. The Captain returned home alone about an hour later. Mrs. Goslett didn't come home to sleep that night.

Next day a man and his son were sailing their model boat

on the Brent River. They discovered the body of a woman floating face downward in the water. The body was identified as Mrs. Goslett. She had been beaten unconscious and thrown into the water.

When informed of his loss, Arthur took the normally traumatic news with unusual calm. The police became suspicious when he couldn't explain the fact that he had made no attempt to find his wife, although she had never stayed out all night before. Police searched the Goslett home and found the shirt Arthur had worn the previous night. It was blood-spattered. They also found his dead wife's earrings, brooch, and handbag, all of which had been in her possession when she was killed.

Arthur confessed to killing his wife. Nasty man that he was, he endeavoured to incriminate Daisy Holt, as if that unfortunate lady didn't have enough problems. Daisy was able to prove that she had had no idea Arthur intended to kill his wife.

Arthur's confession, which was read in court, follows in part:

I was called a coward by Daisy Holt, and she said that if I didn't kill my wife, then someone would kill me. I kept putting her off, but she dared me and said: "There are plenty of places by the river. I suggest you propose taking her to see a house, stun her, and throw her in."

Down by the river I struck her three or four blows. I took the jewellery, and kissed the hand with the wedding ring on, and said I was sorry, and then slung her overboard. I picked up the things and ran home.

The best Arthur's defence attorneys could do was to try to prove that their client was insane. The jury felt that Arthur wasn't insane, just mean. They quickly found him guilty.

Affairs of the heart sometimes defy explanation. As the amorous Captain was led from the Old Bailey, one young lady was seen nearby, sobbing uncontrollably. She was the last person to visit the rascal before he was hanged in Pentonville Prison. She was, of course, his third wife.

ARTHUR, BEATRICE, AND MUMMIE

Arthur Devereux was weird, but he didn't look or act the part. Quite the contrary. Art was a slim, good-looking chemist's assistant who had the ability to turn a young lady's fancy to unladylike actions. Art could charm the birds out of the trees.

One of the birds who came tumbling out was pretty Beatrice Gregory. Beatrice and her Mummie were vacationing in Hastings, England (famous for 1066 and all that) in 1898, when it was Beatrice's dubious fortune to accidentally meet Art. Beatrice fell madly in love and it appears at the outset that Art reciprocated. Despite Mummie's mild objections (for she too thought Art was something of a catch), the couple were married after knowing each other only a few months.

The bloom was soon off the rose. For one thing there was the practical problem of not enough income to provide for anything more than the bare necessities. Then there was Art's attitude. No sooner had the minister blessed the union than Art became a gruff, inattentive companion. To add to the couple's precarious predicament Beatrice found herself, as they used to say, "heavy laden with child."

The arrival of little Stanley only added to the family's financial difficulties. Art tried changing jobs. The Devereux family moved to London. They moved several times, but nothing seemed to change their bad luck. Art began to hate Beatrice, feeling that she was the focal point of all the ill fortune he was enduring. He heaped abuse and insults upon his wife. At the same time, he was abnormally fond of his son Stanley. Nothing was too good for little Stanley. All Art's future plans revolved around his son.

When Beatrice informed Art that she was again pregnant, he became downright nasty. She gave birth to twins. Just as Art had eyes only for Stanley, so Beatrice's affection was turned towards the twins. This directional split of parental affection did nothing to cement relations between the mother and father.

Art now had three individuals to hate instead of one. The grey matter that he employed at the chemist's shop was now almost exclusively occupied with thoughts of his deep-rooted hatred for his wife and the twins. If there were only himself and Stanley everything would be just fine. His income would take care of the two of them adequately. It wasn't his fault that it couldn't be stretched to handle five.

Art had a solution. The first thing he did was to purchase a large trunk. Of all the things Beatrice needed around her sparsely furnished flat, the last thing was a trunk. She meekly inquired as to the wisdom of the purchase. Art replied that he planned to use it for storage of some things that were getting in the way lately. Beatrice refrained from further questions. She had long since acquired the habit of stopping short of arousing Art's trigger temper.

The following evening Art returned from the chemist shop with a bottle of tonic he had promised Beatrice. Unknown to his family he had spiked the tonic with lethal doses of morphine. Beatrice and the twins took large quantities of the spiked tonic. Before retiring for the night Art placed the three bodies into the new trunk.

The next morning Art awoke bright and early. After making a substantial breakfast for himself and Stanley, Art went to Kensal Rise and made arrangements with a moving and storage company to pick up the trunk. He explained that he would be away for some time and wanted the trunk stored for several months. The same afternoon the trunk was picked up.

Art then moved out of his flat and took new lodgings in another part of London. He quit his job and got another. He enrolled Stanley in a private school. Beatrice and the twins were out of sight and out of mind. Art and Stanley were on the threshold of a new life.

Meanwhile, Beatrice's mother, Mrs. Gregory, couldn't locate her daughter. It appeared to her that the entire family had fallen off the face of the earth. After several weeks she managed to trace Art and was amazed that Beatrice and the twins were not with him. Art gave his mother-in-law a story about Beatrice and the twins being in the country, but he wouldn't give her any address.

Mrs. Gregory left the flat and made discreet inquiries around the old neighbourhood. The only unusual thing that had happened was the removal of a large trunk just before Art had changed addresses. Industrious Mrs. Gregory traced down the moving company, went down to their premises, and demanded that the trunk be opened. She then discovered where Beatrice and the twins had been all the time.

Inspector Pollard of Scotland Yard showed up at Art's flat, but the bird had flown. He knew that it was just a matter of time before his mother-in-law traced the trunk. Art settled in Coventry and once again gained employment as a chemist's assistant. Pollard knew that Art would sooner or later seek employment in order to support himself and Stanley. His men were being informed of all applicants for positions in chemists' shops. In this way Pollard was advised of Art's whereabouts.

The Inspector walked into Art's new place of employment and introduced himself. His quarry's first words were, "I don't know anything about a trunk." Inspector Pollard knew he had his man.

Art was arrested and charged with murder. At his trial at London's Old Bailey he claimed that his wife had killed the twins and then committed suicide. When he discovered the bodies he claimed that he had placed them in the trunk, knowing that no one would believe that he had not murdered them. Art was right about one thing – no one believed him. The Crown produced telegrams proving that Art had applied for a new job before Beatrice's death. In his telegram he described himself as a widower with one child.

Arthur Devereux was sentenced to be hanged. The day the sentence was passed in the Old Bailey a middle-aged lady clutched a seven-year-old boy's hand firmly in her own, Mrs. Gregory and her grandson Stanley were all alone.

HE BLEW UP
HIS MOTHER

Recently John Wayne Gacy was convicted of murdering thirty-three young men and boys, thereby becoming the most prolific mass murderer in U.S. criminal history. Twenty-five years earlier another citizen of the U.S. actually murdered a larger number than Gacy. Only a technicality deprived this earlier day monster from being the all-time champ.

John Gilbert Graham first saw the light of day in 1932 in Denver, Colorado. His father passed away when he was only five years old. Left destitute, Jack's mother Daisy had little choice but to place her son in an orphanage, where he remained for six years. In 1943 Mrs. Graham remarried a wealthy rancher, John Earl King and brought her eleven-year-old son to his new home. For a while he was joined by his sister, who later moved to Alaska.

Jack was not a contented child. While he got high marks, he never really showed any interest in school work. He is mainly remembered for an explosive temper, which could flare up at the slightest provocation. When Jack didn't get his way he ran away from home. At the age of sixteen he lied about his age to join the Coast Guard. Nine months later his deception was uncovered and he was dismissed from the service.

Jack returned to Denver and found a job, but quickly

succeeded in getting into trouble. He stole several of his company's blank cheques, forged the name of one of the company's directors, and cashed $4,200 of the bogus paper. With the proceeds he travelled to Texas, where he became a bootlegger. He was apprehended, and after serving a few months in jail was returned to Colorado to face forgery charges. Daisy King stepped in and made restitution in the amount of $2,500, with the firm promise that her son would pay off the balance of $1,700 in installments.

Jack secured work in a garage, married pretty Gloria Elson, and for a while seemed to settle down. The attractive young couple promptly had two children. Daisy doted over her grandchildren.

In 1954 tragedy once again entered Daisy King's life. Her husband Earl died. This time Daisy was left with a comfortable fortune. She decided that her wayward son would reform if given a proper opportunity. Daisy presented Jack with a new home. She would live with her son and daughter-in-law, but the house was in his name. Daisy had also found a drive-in restaurant, which she purchased for $35,000, and asked Jack to run it. No son could ask more of a mother.

But things just didn't work out. Jack always seemed to be short of cash at the end of the day. Daisy couldn't understand how a twenty-three-year-old intelligent boy could not manage to balance his cash with his cash register tapes. Mother and son began to argue over the operation of the restaurant. To relieve the tension, Daisy decided to visit her daughter in Alaska. During October of 1955 she bought Christmas presents to take North.

On Nov. 1, Jack and Gloria, accompanied by their two children, drove Daisy to the airport. Daisy was catching Flight 629 for the first leg of her trip to Alaska. There was a slight delay at the weigh-in counter when it was discovered that her luggage was in excess of the allowable weight of sixty-six pounds. She was over by thirty-seven pounds. When an attendant was told that one suitcase contained Christmas presents he suggested that those items could be mailed a lot cheaper than the twenty-seven dollars he had to charge. Jack would hear none of it. He talked his mother into paying the twenty-seven dollars.

It is to be remembered that there were no security measures at airports twenty-five years ago, but insurance was available from vending machines. Jack sauntered over to the machines and popped in quarters. You could buy $6,250 protection for a quarter. Jack bought several policies, totalling $87,500. His mother joked with him as she signed the policies.

Daisy hugged her grandchildren, kissed her daughter-in-law, and clasped her son to her bosom. Flight 629 took off. Before the Graham family was out of the airport word was received that the DC6B had exploded in mid air. There were no survivors. A total of forty-four men, women, and children had perished. Among them was Mrs. Daisy King.

The F.B.I. lab in Washington quickly ascertained that the plane had been blown up by dynamite. Traces of sodium nitrate and sodium carbonate were found in the gaping torn metal believed to be the location of the internal explosion. The huge hole was located in the baggage compartment.

Authorities could not locate the baggage of one Daisy King, leading them to believe that her luggage may have contained the dynamite. They did find Daisy's handbag, which had been carried aboard the ill-fated plane. In it they found newspaper clippings concerning her son, Jack Graham, who four years earlier had been sought by Denver police as a forgery suspect. F.B.I. agents dug into Jack Graham's life and discovered that he had a penchant for getting into trouble with the law.

Nine days after the disaster F.B.I. agents knocked on Jack's door. He denied any knowledge of the crime. A search of his home uncovered a roll of wire used in connecting up dynamite. Agents also discovered gaily wrapped Christmas presents. Had Jack, unknown to his mother, substituted a dynamite bomb in place of the presents?

After three hours of questioning Jack Graham calmly

changed his story and confessed to perpetrating the horrendous crime. He told the F.B.I. of actually working as an apprentice electrician for ten days so that he could manufacture the bomb without blowing himself up.. He had bought twenty-five sticks of dynamite and all the accessories to construct the bomb. Later clerks in hardware stores identified him as the purchaser of these supplies.

Jack Graham stood trial for the murder of his mother only, thereby escaping the historical notoriety of becoming the greatest convicted mass murderer in U.S. history. After deliberating only an hour and a half, a jury found him guilty of murder in the first degree.

Graham was one of the coolest men ever to be executed. A few days before his date with death he reminded a guard, "If any mail comes for me after next month you can readdress it to hell." On Jan. 11, 1957 he calmly entered Colorado's gas chamber, inhaled deeply, lost consciousness, and was pronounced dead twelve minutes later.

RONALD KILLED
HIS WIFE

Every country has its celebrated murder case – one that becomes indelibly identified with the country in which it was perpetrated. The United States has contributed the Lindbergh kidnapping. Canada produced Albert Guay, while among its galaxy of infamous cases, England's Jack the Ripper stands above the rest. South Africa has given us more than her fair share of unusual cases, but for sheer intrigue and speculation the one case that rises above all the others is the Cohen case.

Isidore Cohen, like thousands of other refugees, fled from Lithuania to escape the oppressive yoke of Czarist Russia. These young men who left Russia before World War I made new lives for themselves wherever they settled. Many eventually had a great influence on their adopted lands in the fields of culture, the arts, and commerce.

Isidore Cohen landed in South Africa at the age of sixteen. He soon mastered the language and opened a small furniture shop in Cape Town. The store flourished. Isidore correctly deduced that the bulging city would expand along the Atlantic seaboard. The sand-covered bushland was considered almost worthless to everyone but Cohen. He invested heavily in the land, gradually gaining ownership of virtually all of Camps Bay, then almost a desert situated about five miles from Cape Town. When Isidore's property was turned into an entire suburb and resort area, land values soared. Cohen became a multi-millionaire.

Isidore married, and sired one son, Ronald. Because he was a self-made man, he insisted that his son make his own mark in life. His boy would be given every opportunity but he would have to make his own fortune. There would be no handouts.

Ronald attended Rondebosch Boys' High School, one of the best schools in Cape Town. He lived with his mother and father in a large, luxurious home in Kenilworth. After attending the University of Cape Town, Ronald, then twenty-five, took a trip to visit a relative in Paris. There he met Marlit Brand, an attractive Hungarian refugee. Ronald and Marlit were married in Sept. 1954. Four years later the couple were divorced. Marlit left Ronald's life as suddenly as she had entered it.

In 1961 Ronald Cohen met beautiful Susan Jonson. He was thirty-two and Susan was seventeen. The pair fell madly in love and wanted to marry immediately. Susan's parents urged Ronald to wait a year until Susan was eighteen. Then, if the lovers felt the same way about each other, they would receive the Jonsons' blessing.

While Ronald was active in affairs of the heart, so too was he busy in the world of commerce. He started out as a clerk in a hardware store, but quickly rose to become an executive of the firm. He branched out until he owned Fletcher and Cartwrights, one of Cape Town's leading department stores. Soon Ronald Cohen's business empire included over a dozen different profitable enterprises. Like his father before him, Ronald became a multi-millionaire while still a young man.

Ronald and Susan were married, and in 1966 Susan gave birth to a son. Unfortunately this child was the victim of an accident, strangling himself in his crib less than a year later.

The Cohens took the death of their son extremely hard, but little by little the pain of their loss subsided. Ronald threw himself into his various business enterprises, becoming a bona fide workaholic. Eventually the Cohens had two more children, who were adored by their parents.

Ronald built one of the finest homes in Cape Town, if not in all of South Africa. Situated on Monterey Drive, it was a huge, sumptuously furnished Spanish-Moorish showplace, equipped with a swimming pool and Persian rugs. Lush formal gardens surrounded the house. Besides Susan, the home was run by a housekeeper-governess, Miss Yvonne Merry, two servants, and a full-time gardener.

The Cohens, with their lovely home, lovely children, and lovely millions, were a devoted, happy couple until the night of April 5, 1970. Miss Merry had gone to bed early. The other servants were asleep in their quarters. Suddenly, Miss Merry, who was lying in bed reading a book, heard Mr. Cohen shouting, "Yvonne! Yvonne! Come quickly." Ronald Cohen appeared in the doorway of her unlocked bedroom. His shirt was covered with blood. "Come quickly," he urged the startled governess. "Someone has broken in."

Once in the library Cohen kneeled beside his fallen wife. Miss Merry noticed with horror that Susan Cohen's head had been crushed. Her nose was a pulpy mass and her jaw had been fractured. Susan had taken a blow behind the right ear with such force that it had nearly severed the ear. Miss Merry made a mental note that the door leading from the library to the terrace was open. Rain was falling outside. Cohen instructed the governess to call the police and then gather up the two children, Jonathan and Jacqueline. Under Cohen's direction, Miss Merry ushered the children into a powder room, the only room in the house without windows. Cohen was obviously afraid that the attacker was still prowling about outside.

The police arrived, and after examining the murder scene, questioned the grief stricken husband. Ronald told the investigating officers that he and his wife had been relaxing in the library earlier that evening. He excused himself and left to use the bathroom. When he returned his wife was struggling in the middle of the room with a blond stranger. Ronald described the intruder as being between twenty-seven and thirty years old, with hollow cheeks, blond hair, and dressed in tan sportswear. Beside himself with a mixture of fear and anger, Ronald grabbed a bronze sculpted ram's head and raced towards the struggling pair. Cohen, surprisingly enough, could not say whether or not he had struck his wife's assailant with the bronze statue. In fact, he could only tell the police that the next thing he remembered was regaining consciousness and finding his wife's body behind a couch.

It was a rather unsatisfactory explanation of a life and death struggle. When questioned about the condition of the stranger's hands, Cohen quickly added that he was wearing gloves. Other than a blood-spattered rug and one overturned chair, the library showed little evidence of a struggle having taken place there. Cohen's arms were badly scratched. He claimed that his wife had inflicted the scratches by mistake during the hectic struggle.

The open door leading from the library to the terrace and gardens beyond was the only way the attacker could have gained entrance to the Cohen home. Police thought the grounds should have shown some evidence of an intruder because the area around the terrace was soft mud. Yet no footprint or scuff marks were found. Someone entering the library would surely have muddy feet. No evidence of mud or dirt was found on the library rug.

Police did not believe there had been an intruder. Ronald Cohen was arrested and charged with the murder of his wife.

While out on bail Cohen had an unnerving experience, or at least he claimed he did. After visiting a tailor in downtown Cape Town, he said he spotted his wife's killer on the street. The killer saw Cohen at precisely the same moment and took off. Cohen gave chase, but lost the man in the crowd. Having lost track of his quarry he asked an elderly lady if she had seen a blond man dash past. The lady answered in the affirmative and directed Cohen up Adderley St. Later, despite advertising for the lady to come forward, Cohen was unable to locate her, and thus lost his one opportunity to prove his story was true.

Cohen later commissioned an artist to paint a picture of the killer from his description. He had the painting widely distributed and offered a substantial reward, but the man in the painting was never located.

On Aug. 24, 1970 Ronald Cohen's murder trial opened in Cape Town. It was one of the most publicized trials ever to take place in South Africa. The entire case boiled down to one question: was Cohen's story of an intruder to be believed, or did he kill his wife and invent the story to avoid punishment?

The presiding judge stated that, taking all the circumstantial evidence in its totality, he could come to no other conclusion than to find Cohen guilty. He added that in his judgement the crime was not premeditated.

The punishment for murder in South Africa is death, unless there are extenuating circumstances. The defence lawyers only had a few days to come up with extenuating circumstances in order to save their client's life. This was no easy task, since Cohen still insisted that he was innocent. Despite this, Cohen's lawyers brought forth psychiatrists who had examined Cohen and found him to be a responsible person whose life was predicated by rules and regulations, which he followed to the letter. As the crime wasn't premeditated, they felt that something had happened in the library that night which compelled Cohen to strike out. As one of them put it: "The ferocity of the attack is indicative of a gross disorganization of his personality. It becomes highly probable that this feral behaviour was unleashed by a sudden confrontation with a catastrophic stimulus. All the actions which occurred during this assault emanated from a person in a state of lowered responsibility."

The judge was greatly influenced by the psychiatrists' reports. Had Cohen wanted to plan his wife's murder he had a gun readily available in his home. Cohen received a sentence of twelve years' imprisonment, which everyone agreed was a far cry from the gallows.

We will never know for sure what happened in the Cohens' library on that rainy night. Only Ronald Cohen knows for sure, and he has never told a living soul.

NASTY MOTHER

There are some murder cases which from the outset quickly lead police to one suspect. Sometimes it is the evidence, and other times nothing more than an overall impression of guilt that limits the investigation to a lone suspect. After all, why go further if the identity of the killer is obvious? Alice Crimmins was that kind of suspect.

Eddie and Alice had been married seven years. The early bickering had led to shouting matches, which usually culminated in one or the other stomping out of their apartment. You see, Eddie and Alice had a basic difference of opinion. Alice, at twenty-six, thought that life was for living. She loved to go out and have a good time. Eddie figured that a woman's place was in the home. It was quite another thing when he stepped out for a few beers with the boys.

The Crimmins agreed to disagree. Eddie moved out of the comfortable Kew Garden Hills apartment in Queens, N.Y. He rented a furnished room about a mile from his former home. Alice and the two Crimmins children, Eddie Jr., five, and Missy, four, remained in the apartment, along with the family dog, a half-spitz named Brandy.

The details of the events that took place on the steaming hot morning of July 14, 1965 have been told by Alice Crimmins hundreds of times. It is her story and she has never varied in its telling. She woke up, washed, dressed, and put on makeup in preparation for a custody hearing concerning the two children. Eddie wanted the children, but Alice had no intention of giving them up.

Once in the past Eddie Jr. had jumped out of his bed in the early hours of the morning and raided the fridge. He overate so much that he became violently ill. Alice had put a stop to that. She installed a simple hook and eye on the children's bedroom door. They couldn't get out of their room until Alice flipped the hook. Usually she could hear the kids laughing and carrying on before she liberated them.

On this morning the room was strangely silent. Alice opened the door. Little Eddie and Missy were gone. Alice called her husband, who immediately phoned the police.

Investigating officers answered what appeared to be a routine call. Two children had probably wandered away from home. They quickly changed their minds. A screen covering the children's window had been removed and was found leaning against the wall of the apartment building. The window itself was cranked open to about seventy degrees. Because of a hole in the screen the window normally was kept closed to keep out insects.

The New York cops, learning of the imminent custody hearing, guessed that one of the parents may have hidden the children. Both parents quickly convinced them that this wasn't the case. It was only a five-foot drop from the window to the ground. Had some demented mind lured the children out of the room, or had they merely wandered away?

The police conducted a massive search. Sound trucks roamed the area, pleading with the children to come out of hiding. Two helicopters scanned open fields for any sign of life. Their task was futile.

Nine-year-old Jay Silverman kicked at some rubbish in a field as he took a shortcut to his home. The rubbish was the body of Missy Crimmins. An autopsy revealed that she had been strangled to death. The hunt continued for Eddie. Five days later Vernon Warnecke and his son were gathering empty beer bottles beside a path in a field. They stumbled upon Eddie's badly decomposed body. The bodies of Eddie and

Missy Crimmins were found about a mile from their apartment, but in opposite directions.

If Alice Crimmins was to be believed, the children had obviously been kidnapped. As their door had been locked from the outside the only exit route was through the window. This did not sit well with the investigating detectives. The window, cranked partially open, wouldn't allow an adult to enter and leave, particularly with one or both of the children in tow. How could one or even two kidnappers cope with the two children? They would never leave their mother willingly in the middle of the night. What was the motive? The Crimmins were not a wealthy family and could not raise any appreciable amount of ransom money. Above all, why hadn't Brandy, who would bark at the slightest disruption in the house, not made a sound while the children were being spirited away?

Police investigated Alice and Eddie Crimmins, and so uncovered the swinging lifestyle Alice was leading. While working as a cocktail waitress Alice, a beautiful woman, had come in contact with high-rolling businessmen and politicians. Investigation revealed that she had several lovers. Under intense and often confidential questioning the men in Alice's life all had one specific comment to make: Alice was fabulous in bed, quite unlike other women these men had known. Under questioning Alice admitted that she had a full and varied sex life.

Alice's estranged husband knew of her wild ways and tortured himself in this knowledge. Once he hooked up a listening device in his wife's bedroom where he could hear every noise from his listening post in the basement. The squeaking of his wife's bed drove him crazy.

Police thought that Alice had murdered her children, probably with the help of a friend. Eddie Crimmins, who cooperated with the police, had an alibi for the night of the killing and was eventually eliminated as a suspect. That left Alice. Had she killed her own children in order to rid herself of the last ties that held her to a life of domesticity? She stuck to her story, but the police looked no further. They couldn't prove Alice was a killer, but they didn't give up trying. Every room in her home was bugged. The phone was tapped and manned by police twenty-four hours a day for two years. Her friends were trailed. Several were harassed into becoming agents for the police.

Two years after the double murder police felt they had enough evidence to bring Alice to trial. She was arrested and charged with the murder of her daughter. Mrs. Sophie Earomirski, who lived in the same apartment complex as the Crimmins, wrote to the police about staring out of her window on the night of the murder. She didn't sign her name to the letter, but police traced her through her handwriting. Mrs. Earomirski was to become the prosecution's star witness.

She swore that on the night of the children's disappearance she couldn't sleep, due to the heat. She went to an open window and saw a man and woman on the street below. The woman had a bundle under one arm and was holding onto a walking child with the other. A dog was trailing the group. The man took the bundle from the woman and tossed it into the trunk of a parked car. Mrs. Earomirski heard the woman say, "My God, don't do that to her." Then they entered the car and drove away. After giving her evidence Sophie Earomirski pointed to Alice Crimmins and positively identified her as the woman on the street that night. Nothing could change her mind.

Thirteen days later the Crimmins jury returned a verdict of guilty of manslaughter in the first degree. Alice received a sentence of from five to twenty years imprisonment. Her attorneys launched a successful appeal, based on the wanderings of three jurors who, contrary to instructions, had taken it upon themselves to visit the murder scene. The trial that followed in 1971 resulted in a verdict of guilty of manslaughter in the death of Missy. In addition, Alice was found guilty of first degree murder in the death of her son. During this trial a former lover stated that Alice had told him she would rather kill the children than give them up to her husband.

Alice was carried, kicking and screaming from the courtroom. Her accomplice in the murder of her children has never been identified.

PART THREE
FROM AROUND THE WORLD

MURDER
DOWN UNDER

Folks down under in Melbourne, Australia, were becoming downright apprehensive. In 1942 they had every reason to believe the seemingly invincible Japanese army would invade their country. Hordes of Allied servicemen were stationed in Australia. Life had taken on a nervous, superficially carefree attitude.

On May 9, 1942, Mrs. Pauline Thompson, the estranged wife of a Melbourne police officer, was found strangled in front of her rooming house on Spring St. A post mortem indicated that tremendous pressure had been applied to Mrs. Thompson's neck by someone with unusually strong hands. Although the victim had not been sexually interfered with, her clothing had been torn to shreds. Mrs. Thompson's handbag was found a short distance away. Her attacker had obviously taken the few pounds the bag contained before tossing it away.

What caused the police concern was the similarity between Mrs. Thompson's murder and that of Ivy Violet McLeod, which had taken place six days previously. Mrs. McLeod, a forty-year-old domestic, was found in a doorway about three miles from her home. Her neck had the same grotesque indentations as those later found on Mrs. Thompson. Although she hadn't been raped, she too had had her clothes ripped into shreds. Both women had been killed where their bodies were found.

Despite the imminent threat of a Japanese invasion, the citizens of Melbourne were well aware that a monster was in their midst. Police could come up with no concrete clues. Nine days later the maniac struck again.

Miss Gladys Lillian Hosking, forty-one, was a secretary employed at Melbourne University. Her body was discovered by a gardener in Royal Park on the morning of May 19, 1942. As in the case of the two previous victims, Miss Hosking's neck had been viciously mangled by someone intent on something beyond cutting off her air supply.

Because of the threat of invasion, an air raid trench had been dug in the park. Distinctive yellow mud had been excavated from the trench. Miss Hosking's body lay face down in this mud. She hadn't been sexually attacked, but her clothing was torn into tiny strips. Miss Hosking's gloves, shoes, handbag, and umbrella were scattered within a ten-yard radius of her body.

Three women had been murdered in strikingly similar circumstances within fifteen days. All were accosted relatively close to their homes. It was obvious that they were not well acquainted with their attacker. He killed on the streets with little regard for his own safety. In the case of Miss Hosking, police surmised that she too had been initially attacked on the street and had been dragged into the park.

Royal Park was located near Camp Pell, at the time an American army installation. Investigating officers, who at this point had come up with little to lead them to the killer, decided that it was possible that the murderer could be an American soldier. Sure enough, they found a guard who remembered a soldier returning to the camp late on the night of Miss Hosking's death. The guard remembered him because he was covered with yellow mud. When casually questioned by the guard, the soldier said he had fallen over a mound of mud while taking a shortcut through the park.

Homicide officers W. Mooney and F. Adam visited Camp

Pell. They slowly walked down rows of canvas tents. When they came to tent number 29 they stopped. There on the ground at the entrance to the tent was evidence of yellow mud. Inside the tent the officers found more of the telltale mud adhering to a metal bed. The officers left the camp, taking mud samples with them. Later their suspicions were verified when laboratory analysis proved that the mud taken from in front of the tent and the bed matched perfectly with mud samples from the freshly dug trench in Royal Park.

The two detectives returned to Camp Pell to interrogate the occupants of tent 29. Before doing so they required clearance from the company commander. He surprised the officers by telling them that he had already received a complaint concerning one of the men in tent 29.

Private First Class Edward Joseph Leonski was continually returning to the camp intoxicated. He caused a disturbance in the tent, babbling incoherently, sleeping fitfully, and waking up in the middle of the night screaming. Once he had inquired of his buddies whether they had ever heard of Dr. Jekyll and Mr. Hyde. During the day he pored over details of the murders that appeared in the newspapers.

The detectives were incredulous that Leonski's tentmates hadn't complained sooner. The soldiers explained that Leonski was such a likeable big guy when sober it was very difficult to suspect him of hurting a fly, let alone of being a vicious murderer.

When Mooney and Adam finally came face to face with their quarry, they knew what the soldiers had meant. Private First Class Eddie Leonski was a well built, tall, blond, twenty-four-year-old with a cherubic face. He was a pleasant good-natured guy, well liked by everyone. He did, however, have the reputation of turning into a real trouble maker when under the influence of alcohol. The guard who had stopped the soldier covered with yellow mud on the night of Miss Hosking's murder picked Eddie out of a line-up of twelve uniformed men.

The police investigated Leonski's background. Born in

New York, Eddie had taken up weight lifting while still a teenager. He had a reputation for having extremely strong hands. Eddie was an honours student who played the piano and sang in the choir. The more police delved into his history the more he resembled an enlistment poster. Eddie exemplified the all-American boy.

Eddie's father had died while he was still a youngster, but his mother had managed to make ends meet and brought Eddie up to be a fine upstanding citizen. Or so she thought. In reality Eddie was overly devoted to his mother. His accomplishments were for her only. His setbacks affected him because he had let his mother down. When Eddie was called into the army he cried at the thought of being separated from his mother.

Once in Australia, Eddie began to drink heavily. While under the influence he would become belligerent and, according to his army buddies, he would undergo a strange transformation. His voice would change dramatically, becoming soft and high pitched, very much resembling a female voice.

Eddie began by picking up girls in Australia. He didn't do anything to them. He just liked to drink with them and listen to them talk. He drank at every opportunity, was often absent without leave and in general was a poor soldier. His army record was in direct contrast to his exemplary behaviour in civilian life.

Eddie himself knew something terrible was happening to him. Once he pleaded with a guard, "Please put me in the guardhouse and keep me there. I'm too dangerous to run around loose!"

Slowly Eddie gravitated from just talking to girls to trying to strangle them. He would release his grip before they lost consciousness. Eddie later explained that he really didn't want to kill the girls. Their voices reminded him of his mother. He only wanted to remove their voices. These girls had reported his attacks to the police, but in each case the attack had taken place in the dark and they were not able to provide useful descriptions.

Eddie couldn't explain why he became a murderer. He didn't know any of his victims, but he had struck a conversation with each of them before clasping his hands around their throats. After killing Mrs. McLeod he knew he had to kill in order to possess the voices of his victims. Eddie couldn't explain his compulsion to rip his victims' clothing. He did say that when he read about his crimes in the newspapers he would cry. Yet, knowing what would happen when he drank, he never hesitated to go on a bender whenever the opportunity presented itself.

Eddie told the authorities of meeting Miss Hosking on the street. He asked her for directions back to camp. She was obliging and walked a way with him. As the hapless woman talked, Eddie knew he had to possess her voice. Without warning, he clutched her throat and, as his victim went limp, he dragged her into Royal Park. It was here that he stumbled and fell on the excavated mounds of yellow mud.

Eddie was examined by psychiatrists. They all agreed that he was full of unnatural feelings for his mother and was undoubtedly a fetishist. However, in the strict legal sense he was found to be sane.

Eddie was tried by a U.S. Military Court, found guilty, and sentenced to death. Just prior to his execution Eddie sang a song in his cell. He sang in a soft, clear female voice.

Edward Joseph Leonski was hanged for his crimes on Nov. 9, 1942.

SCOTCH ROCKS

The Isle of Arran is the largest and most scenic of the Clyde Islands. Situated in the estuary of the River Clyde in Scotland, it has often been referred to as one of the most picturesque locations in the world. Certainly an unlikely spot for murder, but wouldn't you know it – one of Scotland's most notorious murders took place on the side of Goatfell Mountain, Arran's most outstanding feature. Goatfell is a gray cone rising 2,866 feet above sea level.

At the turn of the century the steamer *Ivanhoe* made its way down the Clyde each day, stopping at various ports in Arran. On Friday, July 12, 1889, two young men boarded the *Ivanhoe* at Rothesay. Both were planning to vacation in Arran.

Edwin Robert Rose was a thirty-two-year-old Englishman who was looking forward to two weeks' vacation from his job with a building firm in London. He boarded the *Ivanhoe* in the best of spirits. Edwin wasn't long aboard the steamer when he met a fellow traveller with the same destination. John Annandale and Edwin became friends.

When they reached the port of Brodick, the two men disembarked for the afternoon. The steamer would return for them that same evening. The pair separated in Brodick.

Annandale found it difficult to obtain rooms because a local fair was taking place that week. Finally, he located lodgings at a Mrs. Walker's, who could only provide facilities, such as they were, in a lean-to beside her house. Annandale took the lean-to for a week, informing Mrs. Walker that he and a friend would occupy the premises the following day, Saturday. He would be staying a full week. However, his friend would only be staying until the following Wednesday.

Later that day the men met, boarded the *Ivanhoe*, and returned to Rothesay. Here Rose introduced Annandale to two men he had met during the previous few days, Mr. Thom and Mr. Mickel. All four planned to take the *Ivanhoe* back to Brodick the following day. Rose was delighted that Annandale was able to procure accommodations for them both. The best the two newcomers, Thom and Mickel, could do was to secure lodgings on a boat anchored in the bay.

On Sunday, the men went sightseeing in pairs. That evening all four met and spent the evening together. Over the weekend Thom and Mickel formed an unfavourable opinion of Annandale. They couldn't put their finger on it, but he seemed evasive and uncommunicative about his past. On Monday, when Rose mentioned that he and Annandale would be climbing Goatfell Mountain together, Mickel advised Rose of his intuitive feeling regarding Annandale. Rose shrugged off the warning.

Next day, when Thom and Mickel boarded the *Ivanhoe* to return to Rothesay, Rose and Annandale waved goodbye to them from the pier. The two men then set off to climb Goatfell.

The following morning Mrs. Walker noticed that there was no sign of her two lodgers. She waited until 11 a.m. before entering the lean-to. The skimpy room gave evidence of having been slept in, but the two men were missing. Mrs. Walker assumed that her roomers had skipped without paying the rent.

Rose had been due back in London at his place of employment on Thursday, July 18. He never showed up. Within a few days, relatives of the missing man arrived in Brodick, and after hearing Mrs. Walker's story, contacted the police.

The disappearance became the chief topic of conversation in the area. Soon police, in conjunction with volunteers, formed a search party. In a deep gully covered with granite boulders the search party found the body of Edwin Rose. The dead man had suffered fearful blows to the head, probably caused by a rock. His trousers pockets had been stripped of their contents. Later it was ascertained that Rose had probably been pushed over a precipice. His attacker, realizing the fall had not been fatal, leaned over the fallen man and rained blows upon his head. The missing persons' inquiry had turned into a brutal murder.

Where was the man who had hiked up Goatfell Mountain with Rose? Where was John Annandale?

Police traced Annandale's activities before his meeting with Rose. They found out that before travelling to Arran, he had taken rooms under a fictitious name from a Mrs. Currie of Port Bannatyne. He left wearing a straw hat. When he returned he sported a white yachting cap and brown tennis jacket. During the balance of his stay with Mrs. Currie the wanted man had mentioned that he had climbed Goatfell Mountain. Abruptly one morning he went for a walk and never returned. He stuck Mrs. Currie with his bill, but left two pieces of clothing in his room. The yachting cap and tennis jacket were turned over to the police. They had belonged to Edwin Rose.

Two weeks after the murder, reporters from the North British *Daily Mail* managed to get a handle on John Annandale. His real name was John Watson Laurie of Glasgow. The twenty-five-year-old man was from a well-to-do, respectable family, but had been in and out of minor scrapes all his life. The industrious reporters located a James Aitken, who knew the wanted man as Laurie, and who had been on the *Ivanhoe* with Laurie and Rose. When Aitken first met the two men travelling to Brodick, Rose was wearing a white yachting cap. When he met Laurie after the visit to Brodick he thought it strange that Laurie was now wearing his former companion's cap.

Strangely enough, Aitken met Laurie for a third time in Glasgow after Rose's body was found. He asked Laurie about the case, now referred to by the newspapers as the Arran Mystery. Laurie became flustered and swore the man he had been with was not the same man who was found murdered. Then he dashed away and disappeared into a crowd.

Laurie left his job in Glasgow, walked out on his landlady without paying the rent, sold his pattern maker's tools, and went into hiding. Now actively being sought as a murder suspect under his real name, Laurie wrote his first of several letters. The most wanted man in Scotland wrote his landlady, enclosing his back rent. Suspected murderers usually don't do that. Then again, most murderers don't wear their victim's cap and jacket after the foul deed has been done.

Laurie made his way to Liverpool, where he left several of Rose's shirts in a rooming house that he hastily vacated. He then took the amazing step of writing to the British public by sending a letter to the North British *Daily Mail*. In it Laurie explained that he had left Rose alive and well with two strangers on top of Goatfell.

Laurie's literary talents received wide acclaim throughout Britain. This was better than Robin Hood. No doubt encouraged by the excitement caused by his first letter, Laurie again took pen in hand and dashed off greetings to the Glasgow *Herald*. The letter, published on Aug. 29, filled several pages in an endeavour to convince the public that Laurie was a cross between an angel and a martyr.

On Wed., Sept. 3, over a month after the murder, Laurie was apprehended. A station master became suspicious of a man loitering near the depot. It was Laurie's bad luck that at precisely that moment a constable strolled into the station. Laurie realized what was about to happen. He dashed out, but was tackled in some nearby woods.

Laurie stood trial in Edinburgh for the murder of Edwin

Rose. He pleaded not guilty, claiming that Rose had fallen to his death. He admitted to robbing and then concealing the body. His clean-cut appearance at the trial weighed heavily in his favour. The public had expected a monster, but instead were presented with an articulate young man. Despite this, Laurie was found guilty and sentenced to hang.

Surprisingly, the public didn't want their dashing letter-writing Robin Hood to die. A petition was circulated, pleading for the convicted man's life. Copies were placed in offices, banks, and churches throughout Scotland. The mass petition with 138,140 signatures affixed to it was presented to the Secretary of Scotland. As a result, an order was issued to have Laurie undergo a mental examination. He was found to be of "unsound mind," and the death sentence was commuted to life imprisonment. The convicted murderer was sent to Peterhead Prison to serve his sentence.

Four years later the Arran murderer climbed an eight-foot wall and escaped. He managed to get to a wooded area before guards surrounded him and brought him back. He had been outside the prison compound for only half an hour. It was his last taste of freedom.

John Watson Laurie died in prison on Oct. 6, 1930, at the age of sixty-nine, after serving forty-nine years behind bars.

The crime is still occasionally a topic of conversation in the area. Today there is a cairn marking the spot where Rose's body lay concealed beneath the boulder. A few miles away, in the picturesque village of Sannox, in an ancient graveyard, lies the body of Edwin Rose. The huge granite boulder that serves as a headstone gives no hint of how Rose met his death. The inscription merely states "In loving memory of Edwin R. Rose who died on Goatfell, July 15, 1889."

WHO KILLED
MR. LITTLE?

Mr. Little was a creature of habit. In the years previous to 1858 traces of grey were discernible about his temples. The reliable Mr. Little had slipped gracefully into what the young charitably refer to as the middle years.

As a trusted employee of the Midland and Great Western Railway Co. of Dublin, Ireland for years Little had worked his way up the ladder to the lofty position of chief cashier. Along the way Mr. Little never found time to marry. His work was his life.

Each morning Mr. Little (no one ever called him by anything as familiar as a Christian name) arrived at the three-story director's building of the Dublin Railway Terminus at precisely 10 a.m. While the rest of his staff left promptly at five, Mr. Little would often work well into the night. Even back in 1857 that was considered steady and conscientious.

The afternoon of Nov. 14 was no different from the thousands of afternoons that had preceded it. The female staff left at five, followed by a clerk, Mr. Chamberlain. As was his custom, Mr. Little stayed on to enter the cash receipts for the day into his accounts. Mr. Little was never to leave his office again.

At home, waiting patiently, was his unwed sister. Naturally enough, Miss Little was deeply concerned. Her reliable brother had never been one for nocturnal dalliances of any kind. In fact, he had never stayed out overnight before. Miss Little hardly slept a wink. Next morning she went down to the terminus building to see what had happened to her brother.

Stalking back and forth in front of her brother's office was none other than clerk Chamberlain. He, too, was concerned. It was 10:15 a.m. and Mr. Little had never been late before. Mr. Chamberlain turned decidedly pale when Miss Little informed him that her dear brother had not been home all night. Dear me, thought Chamberlain, could Mr. Little have spent the night in his office?

A carpenter was summoned and easily gained entrance to the office through a glass roof. He opened the door from the inside. Mr. Chamberlain and Miss Little dashed inside. Mr. Little was lying beside his desk in a pool of blood. A neat but gaping incision was evident across his neck, and had served to nearly decapitate the poor fellow. Other wounds, any one of which could have been fatal, were visible about the head. The murder weapon or weapons had been carried away by the killer, who had obviously made his way out of the office through the roof. Mr. Little's key was still in the door. A bloodstained towel had been used to wipe blood from the killer's hands and to clean the blade of a razor and knife that had been used on the hapless Little.

No further clues were uncovered at the murder scene. Of course, at the time, fingerprints had not yet been developed as a means of identification. Investigating authorities at first believed that robbery was not the motive for the murder. There was over a thousand pounds in gold and silver on Mr. Little's accounting table, but upon examining the chief cashier's accounting books, they changed their minds. Over six hundred pounds was missing.

Everyone around the terminus instantly became suspect. One must keep in mind that in those days many railway employees lived in and near the station yard. There was Mr. Hanbury, the stationmaster, and his wife, who made their home on railway property. Another railway employee, Mr. Gunning and his wife, lived with the Hanburys. The Hanburys' servant, Catherine Campbell, was in close proximity to the murder scene on the night Little was killed. This galaxy of suspects served to keep the Dublin police hopping, but did little to identify the killer. In desperation police decided to drain a canal that ran adjacent to the station, under the theory that the killer may have tossed the murder weapon into the canal. It wasn't a bad theory. They came up with a hammer covered with red lead paint. Had the killer used the paint to obliterate bloodstains?

Slowly all the prime suspects were exonerated, and the investigation wound down. The police then decided to wander further afield, and began by questioning all railroad employees, even if it had been established earlier that they had not been in or near the directors' building on the evening of the murder.

The expanded investigation involved the questioning of a man named Spollen. Mr. Spollen had been questioned earlier and dismissed as a suspect. He was employed with the railway as a painter, but had been home with his wife shortly after five on the evening of the murder and could not have been the killer. Detectives couldn't help but notice that Mrs. Spollen had recently undergone a change from being a bright, cheerful woman before the tragedy to her present sullen, nervous state. The transformation was interesting, but had been explained as depression, no doubt caused by the tragic murder of Mr. Little, with whom she had been acquainted.

Despite a large reward offered by the railway for the apprehension of the murderer, nothing further developed for a full six months. Then all hell broke loose. On June 20, 1858, Mrs. Spollen walked into the police station. She stated that she had become a nervous wreck because she knew her husband was the murderer. He had not come home soon after five on the evening of the tragedy. She and her children had lied to the authorities in order to provide her husband with an alibi. In reality Mr. Spollen had arrived home at 7:30 p.m. with a paint bucket full of money taken from Mr. Little's office. Spollen had hidden the money in various caches around the neighbourhood, planning to use it as the occasion arose. He had threatened both his wife and children with death if they breathed a word about his guilt. Mrs. Spollen told the police she knew the various hiding places in which her husband had stashed the money. She led detectives to the locations and, sure enough, the robbery loot was found.

Mrs. Spollen swore that on the evening of the murder her husband had come home with blood on his clothing. He dabbed red lead paint over the bloodstains. She pointed to a section of the canal that hadn't been drained. Mrs. Spollen told police that it was here that her husband had thrown away the murder weapon, his straight razor. When this section of the canal was drained, a razor was found with the name Spollen scratched into the handle. Mrs. Spollen's story had checked out in every detail.

Spollen was arrested and charged with murder. With such strong evidence against him, one would think that Spollen's trial would be routine, but such was not the case. There were complications. The prosecution was hampered by the fact that Mrs. Spollen, by law, could not be a witness against her husband. Corroboration of her evidence by other witnesses was admissible. This law prevented Mrs. Spollen from actually taking the witness stand.

Spollen's four children testified against their father. The children, three boys and a girl, ranging in age from six to seventeen, actually saw their father hide some of the stolen money. They had also been warned by Spollen to remain silent about the whole affair.

You would think that such strong evidence would serve to convince the jury that Spollen was guilty. Not so. The children related their tale as if they had been rehearsed. This may have been the case, but should not have been confused with the truth of what they were saying. It also doesn't sit well with juries to see children giving evidence against a parent.

Despite all the evidence against him, Spollen was acquitted and walked out of court an obviously guilty, but free man. Neither Mrs. Spollen nor her children ever spoke or had anything to do with him again. He was fired from his job at the railway. On the streets of Dublin Spollen was pointed at as an object of derision. Practically driven out of Ireland, he made his way to England and oblivion.

Back in Dublin, a sympathetic public raised enough money to enable Mrs. Spollen and her children to emigrate to the United States.

THE BERMUDA
TERROR

Bermuda is an unlikely locale for murder but, as we all know, the ultimate of crimes knows no boundaries nor class distinction. The semi-tropical paradise, with its bright blue skies and crystal clear water, conjures up images of easy going natives, retired British officers, and playboy millionaires. Homicidal maniacs rarely run amuck in Bermuda. In July of 1958 all this changed.

Mrs. Florence Flood lived outside Hamilton with her taxi driver husband. The attractive thirty-four-year-old was attacked outside her home. She was sexually assaulted and horribly beaten by her attacker. Left for dead, Florence recovered, but was unable to describe her assailant, other than to state that he was young, dark, and thin, which in Bermuda was tantamount to no description at all. The brutal assault was considered by police to be an isolated incident until the following March. This time the victim wasn't as fortunate as Florence Flood.

Mrs. Gertrude Robinson lived alone in a little cottage about a mile from the Flood residence. Gertrude was seventy-two. On the morning of March 7 her naked body was found close by her home. She had been so mercilessly bludgeoned and clawed that witnesses had difficulty identifying the body. No weapon had been used. After raping his hapless victim, the attacker had used his bare fists to beat the life from the frail elderly widow.

This second brutal attack crystallized the fact that a madman was loose on the island. The sale of every conceivable type of lock soared. Citizens purchased watchdogs and revolvers, but most realized that if a cunning, depraved sex maniac was at large, he would sooner or later find a woman alone. Police seemed helpless as the attacker had left no clues, no footprints, no fingerprints, and had used no weapon other than his hands.

Nine weeks passed. On May 11, the Bermuda rapist struck again. Dorothy Pearce was the divorced wife of a Royal Navy officer. She lived alone in a cottage facing the sea. Her immediate neighbour thought it strange that he hadn't seen the elderly woman for over two days. When he strolled next door to investigate he found two full milk bottles outside Dorothy's locked door. He called the police.

The police broke down the door and entered the cottage. Mrs. Pearce's body was found in a pool of blood in her bedroom. The brutality of the attack was evident from the swollen and beaten condition of the nude corpse. Again the maniac had used nothing but his bare hands, nails, and teeth to kill the victim. As in the previous cases, cash and jewellery had been ignored.

Six weeks later, the Bermuda Terror, as he was now called by the press, struck again. Rosaleen Kenny lived in the same general area as the three previous victims. One night she woke up and, to her horror, spotted the figure of a man ready to pounce upon her bed. Paralyzed with fear, Rosaleen screamed. A young couple who occupied the second floor of the two-story home heard her screams and rushed downstairs. The intruder heard them coming and loosened his grip on his victim. Then he let go altogether and ran out the open front door into the night. Rosaleen's description of the madman was understandably vague.

Dorothy Barbara Rawlinson was twenty-nine, an attractive English woman who had first visited Bermuda for a vacation. Dorothy loved the island so much she never left. Because she was a fully trained secretary she had no difficulty finding employment. Dorothy lived with Anne and Thomas Sayres in Pembroke, near Hamilton. On her two days off, Thursday and Sunday, she loved to sunbathe. Dorothy had received permission from a retired army officer to sunbathe on Southlands Beach, which he owned.

On Sun., Sept. 27, Dorothy cycled down to Southlands Beach as usual. She never returned. As the hour grew late the Sayres discussed calling the police. They decided to wait until morning. Next morning Thomas Sayres, accompanied by police officers, went down to Southlands Beach looking for Dorothy. The windswept beach was deserted. The wind had smoothed out any tracks that may have been there the night before. Dorothy's bicycle was found lying in the sand.

Police found some blood splattered rocks. That was enough. They returned with twelve officers, equipped with shovels. Soon the beach was criss-crossed with trenches. The officers uncovered Dorothy's wristwatch, green shorts, and white blouse.

Next day frogmen searched the shoreline, but still found no trace of Dorothy. A half mile away, seventy-year-old Frederick Astwood was fishing from his rowboat in a sheltered cove. He found what was left of the battered, half-eaten body. Doctors were able to distinguish which wounds had been inflicted by sharks and which had been inflicted by Dorothy's killer.

All the Bermuda Terror victims had met their deaths in Warwick Parish, a one-square mile of Bermuda that was now practically deserted after dark. Yet it was believed that the latest victim had been killed during daylight hours. Why was no one seen coming to the beach or leaving? The entire Bermuda police force of 150 men were now working on little else.

Police Superintendant Lodge asked Scotland Yard for help. The Yard responded by sending Detective Superintendent Richard Lewis and Detective Sargeant Fred Taylor to Bermuda.

The Scotland Yard detectives were successful in locating witnesses who remembered seeing Dorothy sunbathing just before 5 o'clock on Sunday. Others swore that she wasn't there at 5:45. Someone had committed the crime during that three quarters of an hour span. The detectives felt that after the killer had raped and murdered, he had carried the body into the sea, hoping the sharks would obliterate all traces of his crime. They thought it reasonable to search for anyone who had been seen with wet clothing around the time of the murder.

The two detectives re-enacted the crime. They figured the killer had followed the shoreline after depositing the body in the sea. Lewis and Taylor followed the beach until they came to an area overgrown with brush. Upon examining this wooded area they uncovered a trail. The trail led to a road, which took them to a golf course. Here the detectives questioned a shopkeeper whose store had been open on the day of the murder. Sure enough, he remembered one particular customer that day – because the man's clothing was wet. The young man often bought cigarettes from the shopkeeper and sometimes caddied at the golf course.

Within an hour the two Scotland Yard detectives were in front of the dilapidated shack of nineteen-year-old Wendell Willis Lightbourne. At first Lightbourne denied any knowledge of the crime. Then he admitted to having been near the beach fishing, and finally he confessed to talking to the girl, but swore he left her unharmed, sunbathing on the beach.

Lightbourne was arrested and charged with the murder of Dorothy Rawlinson. As his trial unfolded he emerged as a rather pathetic figure, who could neither read nor write. Sometimes he caddied to make a little money. At other times he did whatever menial tasks he could find. He told of an uncontrollable urge to inflict pain on the opposite sex. He did not know the women he had attacked and had no personal reasons for harming those particular women. They just happened to be in the wrong place when his uncontrollable urge came over him.

Lightbourne was found guilty of murder, with a recommendation for mercy. Despite the rider on his sentence, he was condemned to death. In January 1960, this sentence was commuted to life imprisonment. As there are no prisons in Bermuda capable of housing a convicted killer, Lightbourne was transported to England to serve his sentence.

THE FRENCH
CONNECTION

In the hot and humid climes of South America, tempers sometimes flare with little provocation, resulting in murder most foul. In the United States, violent sick rampages by violent sick men have recently been the rule rather than the exception. England has always produced its intriguing, weird murders.

Ah, but for crimes of passion and affairs of the heart, we must turn to the French. Innovative triangles and other strange permutations too risqué to even whisper about have always been identified with the passionate inhabitants of France.

Mademoiselle Gabrielle Bompard was not a classic French beauty. Her countenance had a stern hardness to it that detracted from her even, chiselled features. But Gaby had an hourglass figure: an ample bosom and a waist so tiny as to be sinful; well proportioned hips that tapered down to a perfect pair of long lean legs.

Gaby was a prostitute in Lille. Finding the pickings too slim for her liking, she looked for greener pastures and, like many others, she headed for Paris. The year was 1890, and Gaby found, much to her dismay, that her chosen profession was overcrowded with women who were as well stacked as she.

Times were tough, but a ray of sunshine was just around the corner. The ray's name was Michael Eyraud, whose main occupation was a never-ending search for the ways and means of avoiding work. A tall, thin man with a full beard, Michael was a small-time punk and petty thief. He took one look at the voluptuous Gaby and thought to himself, that's for me. The twenty-two-year-old pro and the small-time punk became – first things first – lovers, and then partners in crime.

Gaby hung out in the better class bars. Balding, middle-aged men, with wallets bulging like their tummies, were enticed to the apartment, where Michael relieved them of their overstuffed wallets. Most were in a position where they could ill afford to report the robbery to police. Gaby and Michael made their precarious living in this way for months.

Just when the villainous pair turned their thoughts to murder we do not know. What we do know is that they picked as their first victim a solicitor named Gouffe. This unfortunate gentleman made pursuing the opposite sex his main activity in life. Gaby lured him to her apartment many times. Michael resisted the urge to take his money and call it a day. He and Gaby knew that Gouffe was supposed to have a large amount of cash in his office safe. He always carried the keys·to his office and safe on his person.

Michael set the scene for their rather original plan. He rented a posh room in the Rue Tronson-Ducoudry. Gaby informed Gouffe that she had procured new lodgings. Soon he would be invited over to enjoy the new digs. Gouffe could hardly wait.

Meanwhile, back at the new room, Michael had set up a quaint little pulley system. The room had a rather large alcove, enclosed by a curtain. Gaby's bed was just outside this curtain. A pulley with a rope threaded through it had been fastened to the ceiling. One end of the rope was hidden behind the curtain, while the other end hung innocently down the outside of the curtain, falling beside the bed. This end was equipped with a small hook.

Before inviting Gouffe up to the room, Gaby and Michael took a trip to London, England, where they purchased a large trunk. Then the big night arrived. Gouffe, his mind full of things sexual, took the steps leading to Gaby's apartment two at a time. Gaby greeted him at the door, clad in a nightgown. Holding a bottle of wine in her right hand, she waved the anxious Gouffe into the room.

It is difficult to say whether Gouffe died happy, or whether he realized at the very end that something was amiss. As they sipped their wine, the lovers sat down on the bed. Gaby untied the cord of her nightgown. Teasing her lover, she drew it around his neck and fastened it securely. In a flash, Michael tiptoed from behind the curtain, attached the hook to the nightgown cord, and gave a mighty pull on his end of the rope. Voilà, Gouffe rose as if by magic, and without a sound was hanged.

Next morning the body was placed in the waiting trunk and taken to a wooded area near the village of Irigny, near Lyons. Once back in Paris Michael dashed to Gouffe's office to gather up the loot. He had no trouble gaining entry to the office, but try as he might, he couldn't open the safe. In disgust he left empty-handed. Ironically he missed a large sum of money in a box sitting on the victim's desk. Michael and Gaby had gained nothing by becoming murderers. The whole thing was a terrible mistake. They panicked and fled to the United States.

Denis Coffy was working repairing the road near Lyons. After his noon-day lunch, he stumbled upon the decomposed body of the unfortunate Gouffe.

Because he had already been reported missing to the Paris police, it wasn't long before Gouffe was identified. A photograph and description of the trunk was widely published throughout Europe. A clerk in Schwartiger's shop in Euston Rd. spotted the picture and immediately recognized the trunk he had sold. The transaction was clear in his mind because the couple who had bought the trunk were French. He gave the police a perfect description of Gaby and

Michael. Soon the pair were being sought as prime suspects in the murder case.

Gaby couldn't stand the good old U.S.A. For one thing, no one spoke French. She returned to face the music. Michael had made his way to Cuba, where a Frenchman stood out like an elephant at a flea circus. Michael was taken into custody and returned to France.

During the early winter of 1890, France, and indeed much of Europe discussed little else than the sensational trial of Gaby and Michael. To make matters more dramatic, the partners in crime blamed each other for the unique murder.

In the end both were found guilty. Gaby received twenty years' imprisonment, but was released after having spent less than half that time behind bars. Michael lost his head to the guillotine.

PART FOUR
MERRIE ENGLAND

THE JUSTICE MINISTER WAS A KILLER

Thomas John Ley was not your typical murderer. Then, John McMain Mudie was not your average victim, either. You see, Mr. Ley was the wealthy former Minister for Justice of New South Wales, Australia; Mudie was an English bartender. The tale of these two men, and how one killed the other, without ever exchanging a word of conversation, has been described by the Lord Chief Justice of England as one of the strangest cases ever presented to an English jury.

Ley was born in England but moved to Australia when he was eight years old. While still in his twenties he became deeply involved in politics. In 1922, at age forty-one, after a gradual climb up the political ladder, he became Minister of Justice. For years the Hon. Thomas Ley was one of the most influential men in Australia. With power came wealth. Ley was the director of several large companies, but left Australia for England in 1928, hurt because he hadn't been chosen Deputy Premier when the Prime Minister visited Europe.

Thomas Ley's wife was unaware that he supported a mistress for over twenty years. Mrs. Brooks was a widow, whose daughter was married to an Englishman named Barron. When Ley went to England he took Mrs. Brooks with him, leaving his wife behind in Australia. Strangely enough, Ley ceased having intercourse with Mrs. Brooks after returning to England. In fact she acted as Ley's housekeeper and companion in the twelve years prior to the Mudie murder.

Mrs. Brooks' daughter required an operation. Ley suggested that Mrs. Brooks move in with her son-in-law while her daughter was convalescing in hospital. The Barrons lived on Homefield Rd. in London in a house of flats operated by a Mrs. Evans.

One of the roomers at Homefield Rd. was John Mudie, a bartender who, as the saying goes, never did anyone any harm. From all reports Mudie was a decent, hardworking, quiet man. Mrs. Evans spoke highly of Mudie and doted upon the only bachelor residing in her establishment. Sometimes she tidied up his rooms. In return Mudie was most obliging in running errands for his landlady. Occasionally John Ley dropped over to the Evans' establishment to have tea with Mrs. Brooks. In this way he met Mrs. Evans.

It is not our function to analyze people's minds, but certainly the obsession which was to overtake, envelop, and eventually ruin John Ley defies explanation. Later, psychiatrists would conveniently decide the successful businessman and politician was suffering from paranoia. Whatever the reason, Ley became obsessed with the idea that John Mudie was carrying on a torrid love affair with the sixty-six-year-old Mrs. Brooks. He became insanely jealous of the entire fictitious relationship. Mrs. Evans was to state that Mudie met Mrs. Brooks only once, and that was in her company, on a stairway where the three passed the time of day for a moment or two.

The seed of insane jealousy firmly planted, Ley proceeded to hatch a diabolical plot to murder Mudie, who was in all probability the most innocent victim of any premeditated murder ever committed.

Ley approached a hotel porter named Minden at the Royal Hotel in Woburn Place. Minden knew Ley as a solicitor and a former guest of the hotel who in the past had visited with his wife from Australia. Ley inquired of Minden if he knew of a man with a motor car who could be trusted, letting the porter know that such a man could earn as much for one piece of work as he normally would in an entire year.

Minden, assuming that the vehicle was to be used by the solicitor for legitimate purposes, put Ley in contact with an acquaintance, William Buckingham. Minden received ten pounds from Ley for the favour.

Ley and Buckingham met and for the first time Ley told someone else of his intentions. He alleged that a young man had seduced a mother and daughter and was now blackmailing the two women. It was Ley's plan to kidnap the young man and give him a good scare. Then he would provide him with a sum of money and force the culprit to leave the country. Ley promised he would pay Buckingham well for his assistance. He told Buckingham that another accomplice in the scheme, Lawrence John Smith, a carpenter, would eventually meet with them to iron out the details.

The following evening the former Minister of Justice, the man with the car for hire, and the carpenter met at the Royal Hotel to finalize their plans. Buckingham suggested bringing a friend of his, Mrs. Lillian Bruce, into the plot in order to lure the victim into a car on his way to Ley's residence at 5 Beaufort Gardens. Buckingham was so enthused with the promise of easy money that he brought his son into the scheme as well.

In fairness to all the conspirators, it is quite possible that at this time, they believed Ley's story. When Minden suggested that Buckingham had a car for hire he asked if it would be used for legal purposes. Mrs. Bruce also inquired if anything asked of her was illegal. All received assurances from Ley that as a solicitor he was operating well within the law.

And so all the characters of the diabolical plot are now in position – Ley, Buckingham, his son, Mrs. Bruce, and of course the bartender at the Reigate Hill Hotel, the unsuspecting John Mudie.

Mrs. Bruce, posing as a well-to-do customer, made it a point to become acquainted with the pleasant, unassuming Mudie. It wasn't difficult. Young Buckingham posed as her chauffeur. Eventually Mrs. Bruce asked Mudie if he would care to earn some extra money working as a bartender at a cocktail party she was giving on the evening of Nov. 28, 1946. Mudie jumped at the opportunity.

On the appointed night young Buckingham and Mrs. Bruce picked up Mudie at the Reigate Hill Hotel for the ride into London. Young Buckingham drove his father's Wosley. Unknown to Mudie, another vehicle, a Ford, licence number 101, which had been rented a week earlier by Smith, preceded the Wosley to 5 Beaufort Gardens. Smith and his passenger, Buckingham Sr., entered Ley's residence.

Mrs. Bruce, young Buckingham, and Mudie entered 5 Beaufort Gardens. Young Buckingham merely opened the door and returned to the car. Once the victim was delivered, Mrs. Bruce's work was done. She excused herself, saying she had to consult with her chauffeur. As the door closed behind her, the senior Buckingham and Smith threw a carpet over poor Mudie's head. He was gagged and firmly tied with rope.

Exactly what went on behind the closed door will never be known for sure. Young Buckingham and Mrs. Bruce drove to the Crown and Sceptre for a few drinks. Buckingham and Smith were supposed to join them. Only the elder Buckingham showed up.

Meanwhile the terrified Mudie sat with a carpet tied firmly over his head with no idea of what was happening to him. Smith remained in the room. Ley, his brain racing in ecstacy, had managed to pull it off. After all the scheming and plotting, his supposed antagonist was trussed up and helpless before him.

*   *   *

On Nov. 29, 1946, Walter Coombs of Woldingham, Surrey, was walking home after finishing work. It was he who discovered the body of John Mudie in a chalk pit. Death was the result of strangulation with a rope, which was tied around the neck. John Mudie's body was identified immediately. His killers had overlooked his personal card in his pocket.

Buckingham and Mrs. Bruce read about the terrible conclusion to the kidnapping plot in the newspapers. The chalk pit murder, as it became known, received wide publicity.

Buckingham and Mrs. Bruce went directly to the police and told the whole story, but insisted that when they left Mudie he was definitely alive. A gag and pick axe found at the scene of the crime were later traced to 5 Beaufort Gardens.

When the entire plot unfolded Smith and Ley were charged with murder. All the other participants turned King's evidence and were never tried.

As the architect of the murder there was little doubt as to Ley's guilt. Smith claimed that the last time he saw Mudie he was alive. The evidence of two alert citizens proved that, unlike his fellow conspirators, Smith knew that Mudie was to be murdered, not merely kidnapped.

Clifford Tamplin and Fred Smith, two landscape gardeners, were cycling past the chalk pit on Nov. 27, the day before the murder. They were startled to notice a car parked in the desolate area. As they came upon the scene a man appeared some distance inside the pit. When the man spotted the cyclists he dashed wildly to his car and quickly drove away. The two men noted the licence plate number – 101 – and the make of the vehicle, a Ford.

Later, when they heard a body had been found at that exact spot on Nov. 29, they went to the police with their story. As the killing was definitely committed on the 28th, using a Ford car with licence plate number 101, their story proved that Smith, who had rented the car earlier in the week, was reconnoitering the location to dump the body the day before the murder took place. This proved he had prior knowledge that murder was to take place.

Both Ley and Smith were found guilty of murder and sentenced to death, although it was never established which one actually stranged John Mudie. Later their sentences were commuted. Smith was given a sentence of life imprisonment, while Ley was judged insane and sent to Broadmoor, where he was one of the wealthiest men ever to be incarcerated in that institution. Three months later the Hon. Thomas John Ley, former Minister of Justice of New South Wales, suffered a stroke and died.

NOT WITH MY SISTER

It is a source of amazement to me that in recent times there has been a drought of honest-to-goodness bigamists. Has this art form gone the way of hula hoops, stained glass windows, and chimney sweeps? Where are those dapper gentlemen who led double lives, not for weeks or months, but for years?

Indeed, to resurrect one such rogue for your reading pleasure, it is necessary to turn back the calendar to 1892 and visit with James Canham Read, who lived in assorted towns and villages close by London, England. Jimmy was tall, dark, and handsome. He was also a real rascal when it came to his relationships with the opposite sex. Jimmy didn't just lead a double life. Our boy Jimmy had four on the string at one time.

Let's see now, there was the original Mrs. Read, a loyal homebody who tended to the washing and cleaning. Mrs. Read didn't have that much choice. As the mother of eight little Reads she rarely had time to enjoy herself. It is disheartening to relate that Mrs. Read, despite her more than adequate domestic contribution to the care and comfort of the main character in our little drama, had absolutely nothing else to do with the entire affair. I understand she cried a lot.

In August 1892, Jimmy just happened to bump into Mrs. John Ayriss, a tiny but well-endowed mother of four healthy strapping children. It wasn't long after their initial chance encounter that Jimmy was having encounters of a sexual kind with Mrs. Ayriss.

One can't help but wonder how Jimmy financed his affairs, being all the while employed as a clerk at the Royal Albert Docks at a salary of £140 per annum. Even before the turn of the century this sum was not a fortune.

One fine day in September handsome Jimmy and Mrs. Ayriss were taking a leisurely stroll on Clapham Common, when who should they bump into but Mrs. Ayriss' younger sister Florrie. As any dutiful sister would, Mrs. Ayriss introduced Florrie to her friend Jimmy Read. You guessed it; Jimmy took one look at Florrie, who was a knockout, and decided then and there that two sisters were better than one.

It was only a matter of weeks before Jimmy initiated Florrie into his stable of willing lovers. From the last half of 1893, well into May of 1894, Jimmy bedded down with his wife, Mrs. Ayriss, and Florrie at every opportunity, but not necessarily in that order. It appears that Florrie, who lived in Sheerness, may have been his favourite.

Although Jimmy and Florrie were careful to keep their relationship secret, Mrs. Ayriss found out about the unfaithful Jimmy and her own sweet sister Florrie. She smouldered from within, but there was little she could do. When you are unfaithful to your own husband it is difficult, if not impossible, to blow the whistle on your lover for rolling in the hay with your sister.

In the midst of all this intrigue, Jimmy found himself one day innocently partaking of some sweets in a confectionary store. He sampled a Turkish delight and found it to his taste. Jimmy, who never stopped hustling, also found the sweet young woman who served him to his liking. Miss Kemper soon became Jimmy's fourth partner in sex. The innocent purveyor of sweets knew Jimmy as Edgar Benson, a commercial traveller. She was soon ensconced in an apartment which she shared with Jimmy, never knowing that she was only one of four.

Tending to the sexual desires of all four ladies was tiring, time-consuming, yet enjoyable. Then Jimmy received a decidedly distressing piece of information from Florrie. "I am going to have a baby and it's yours," she said.

This unsettling bit of news did not go over well with Jimmy. For one thing, if Mrs. Ayriss found out, as she undoubtedly would, there would be the devil to pay. Besides, Jimmy felt he had enough children already. No, definitely no. Florrie had to go.

Jimmy then proceeded to swing into action. On June 24, 1893, he met with Florrie to talk over their embarrassing predicament. The couple went for a stroll hand in hand near the village of Prittlewell, just north of Southend. Jimmy simply produced a revolver and shot Florrie in the head. He then threw her body over a hedge and returned via a well-used footpath. In order to obscure his trail Jimmy walked all night toward London. At 8 a.m. Monday morning he called on a friend at Leyton, washed, shaved, and had breakfast. By 10 a.m. he was at his office at the Royal Albert Docks.

Whatever else Jimmy was, he was not a dunce. He realized that at some point he would be questioned about Florrie's death. He needed to disappear. With this thought in mind, Jimmy opened his employer's safe and took £160, more than his salary for an entire year, and left his office. He went to Rose Cottage at Mitcham, where the lovely Miss Kemper waited with open arms. Jimmy planned on permanently becoming Mr. Edgar Benson, commercial traveller.

Elsewhere the universe was unfolding. Florrie's body was found that same Monday. A medical examination revealed that the murder victim was in an advanced state of pregnancy. Her identity was immediately established as Florrie Dennis. Mrs. Ayriss had reported her sister missing when she was unable to locate her on Monday morning.

Jimmy spent the next four days at Rose Cottage, but it was no use. Now a robbery suspect, as well as a possible murderer, Jimmy was traced to his love nest. On June 29, Scotland Yard detectives showed up at Rose Cottage and arrested Jimmy Read.

On Nov. 13, 1894, Jimmy Read stood trial for murder. The Crown presented a formidable circumstantial case. Jimmy had sent Florrie a wire setting up their last meeting. He was identified by a Mrs. Kirley as being near the scene of the murder on the fateful Sunday. Another witness, a Mr. Douthwaite, testified that he saw the accused man walking with Florrie close to the hedge where the body was later found. Several witnesses, including a constable, identified Read as the man who inquired about directions to London during the early hours of the morning of Monday, June 25. Even Miss Kemper revealed the facts surrounding Jimmy's appearance at Rose Cottage on the Monday following the crime. He urged her to fetch papers featuring the murder, was nervous, and hardly left the tiny cottage for four full days.

In an attempt to counteract this testimony, the defence pointed out that there was no real evidence that Jimmy was the father of Florrie's unborn child. The prosecution had been unable to come up with a murder weapon and had failed to prove that Jimmy had ever owned one.

Despite this, the Read jury deliberated only a half hour before finding Jimmy guilty of murder. All appeals failed. James Canham Read professed his innocence right up to the time he was hanged on Dec. 4, 1894 in Springfield Prison, Chelmsford.

WHOLESALE
SLAUGHTER

We are all familiar with that nasty gentleman known as Jack the Ripper, who held London, England in a state of terror during the autumn of 1888. Jack passed his time murdering and mutilating prostitutes. His true identity remains a mystery to this day. Earlier in the nineteenth century, another man terrorized London, keeping its inhabitants in much the same state of fear as the Ripper, but his murders are not nearly as well known. This may be because his identity was established at the time, removing the element of mystery from his dastardly deeds.

Mr. and Mrs. Marr had worked hard to build up their dry goods store in London's rough, tough east end. Sailors from around the world wandered the street in 1811 looking for hard drink and loose women. Seagoing voyages lasted months, and who was to blame a man for letting off a little steam when he hit port? Mr. Marr had been a sailor for years before deciding to save his money, marry, and settle down to the life of a shopkeeper. His shop, located at 29 Ratcliff Highway, prospered.

The Marrs had an infant daughter, a fourteen-year-old apprentice, and a servant, seventeen-year-old Margaret Jewell, on the premises. Mrs. Marr was pregnant. On this particular day, Sat. Dec. 7, she had a craving for something unusual to eat. She asked Margaret to fetch some oysters at a nearby fish shop. Margaret left on her errand at closing time, 11 p.m.

It was a dark, foggy night. The streets were full of carousing drunken sailors. Margaret tried two different fish shops, but the hour was late and they were closed. Giving up, she returned to the Marr's shop, which she found locked and in darkness. This was strange, as Mr. Marr had promised to leave the door ajar for her. Margaret, somewhat apprehensive, pounded on the door. Finally, a neighbour, Mr. Murray, came to her rescue. He told the frightened girl that he would go to the back of the shop and try to gain entrance from the rear. When he got there, he was surprised to find the back door wide open. A lone candle cast an eerie shadow across the back room of the shop. Murray cautiously entered the building.

He found Mr. Marr lying in a pool of blood behind the shop counter. His head had been smashed in with one vicious blow. Someone had then leaned over the fallen man and cut his throat from ear to ear. Murray came across the bodies of Mrs. Marr and the apprentice in the same room. They too had had their throats slit in the same manner. The hysterical man made his way through the carnage to the front door and let in Margaret Jewell and the small crowd that had gathered. The baby was found in her room. Her throat had also been slashed.

Margaret promptly fainted and had to be carried from the shop.

The only clues to the madman's identity was a heavy bloodied mallet found at the scene, which bore the initials J.P. The inhabitants of the east end were accustomed to brawls and beatings, but this was different. An entire family, including an innocent infant, had been wiped out in twenty minutes. Could such a madman strike again?

Twelve days passed. Mr. Williamson, the proprietor of a public house, The King's Arms, was no longer a young man, but he was tough and hard. The King's Arms was located in the same general neighbourhood as Mr. Marr's dry goods shop.

This Thursday evening was no different than the thousands that had preceeded it. At closing time, 11 p.m., Williamson's customers began drifting off into the foggy night. Mrs. Williamson and a waitress helped clean up. A granddaughter was peacefully asleep in a bed upstairs. A young carpenter named Turner, who lived at The King's Arms, strolled in and continued on straight up to his room.

At precisely 11:25 p.m. Turner sat bolt upright in his bed. A bloodcurdling scream rang through the building. Turner immediately thought of the recent murders in the neighbourhood. He slowly got out of bed and quietly walked to the landing, which afforded him a view of the scene below through an open door. He perceived a tall man bending over Mr. Williamson's body. When the man straightened up to rifle the cash drawer, Turner heard the stranger's boots give a distinctive creak.

He waited no longer. Quaking with fear, for Turner was sure the assailant would search the bedrooms and kill him, he decided to escape. Fastening his bedclothes into a rope, he lowered himself out of his bedroom window. The rope was too short. Poor Turner was found dangling there with no place to go by passersby.

He told his terrifying story, and in a few minutes several neighbours entered The King's Arms. Mr. and Mrs. Williamson and their servant were dead. They had each received a solitary blow to the head, after which the murderer had slit their throats, with one vicious well-practiced slash. The group of neighbours apprehensively walked up the stairs to the granddaughter's bedroom, not daring to think what might await them. The eleven-year-old child was unharmed. She had slept through the entire slaughter.

Thousands of handbills describing the tall man with the creaking boots were distributed throughout London. The handbills also mentioned the mallet with the initials J.P. One of these handbills came to the attention of a lodging house proprietor named Virmiloe. He recognized the mallet as belonging to a lodger of his named John Peterson. His lodger's tool chest was examined and the mallet was missing, but Peterson had been at sea for weeks and could not have been the killer.

Another lodger, John Williams, immediately came under suspicion. Fellow lodgers remembered that on the night of both murders Williams had come in late. He always had plenty of money, but never worked. Recently he had purchased a new pair of boots, which squeaked loudly whenever he walked. Williams was a good-looking, pale man with bright yellow curly hair. He was blunt with fellow roomers, and not at all well liked.

There was little doubt that Williams was the earlier day Ripper. Once taken into custody and well aware of the fate awaiting him, Williams made a noose of his bedclothes and hanged himself in his cell. In keeping with the barbaric customs of the times, his body was placed on view to the public before a stake was driven through his heart.

Six weeks after his death a blood-encrusted dagger was found in Williams' room at his lodging house. He had stuffed it into a mousehole in the wall just before he was taken into custody.

WAS HE GUILTY?

The trap door springs open and the convicted killer plunges to eternity. Later it is distressing to learn that the executed man may not have been a killer at all. In hindsight a reasonable doubt has crept in. Could the prisoner's protestations of innocence have been sincere? Did an innocent man hang?

Jane and Henry Dobson owned a farm about a quarter of a mile from the tiny village of Wolviston, England. The farm, known as High Grange, afforded the Dobsons a comfortable living. Besides the main house on the farm, another dwelling was usually occupied by a farm labourer and his family.

On Jan. 18, 1938, Jane Dobson left High Grange heading for Wolviston. She never made it. When she failed to return that evening Henry Dobson rationalized that his wife may have continued on to Newcastle to visit their married daughter. That night he made three trips down from the farmhouse to the road to meet the bus, but each time there was no sign of his wife.

Next morning at 9:35 a.m. he decided to walk into the village. Taking a shortcut across a farm track, he noticed a crumpled object lying just off the path, partly in some grass and partly in a plowed field. He found his wife's body. Stunned, he circled the body for a few moments and then took off for the village to summon the police.

95

An autopsy was performed by pathologists at Sunderland Royal Infirmary. Mrs. Dobson had been viciously raped. She had been stabbed directly into the chest and neck. Either of the two stab wounds would have resulted in death. The victim had also been beaten about the head before expiring.

Who would do such a thing? The presence of strangers in the isolated farming district would be conspicuous. The victim was a hard-working honest farmer's wife. She had no bad habits, didn't drink, nor had she any male friends outside her own family.

Police questioned Mr. Dobson, who at first could not recollect one single enemy. Searching his memory he recalled that several years before he and his wife had had a rather bitter argument with the hired hand who lived on his farm at the time. The man's name was Hoolhouse. Dobson had ordered the family off his property. They had left, but still lived nearby in Haverton Hill, about four miles from High Grange. At the time of the incident the Hoolhouses had a son, Robert, who was now a strapping twenty-year-old.

In the meantime police were endeavouring to trace Mrs. Dobson's last walk. According to Mr. Dobson's statement, his wife left the farm between 4:30 and 5 o'clock. At about 5:30 Percy Swales and Thomas Nelson drove their cattle truck off the road onto the farm track. It was dusk. Their headlights picked up a man standing beside the road. The man quickly dropped to the plowed field. The stranger's obvious mode of travel was a bicycle, which was lying beside the road.

Swales drove up to the man and shouted, "Hullo, what's the game here?"

The man replied in an easily distinguishable local accent, "I'm all right. I have had one over the nine. Drive on." Loosely translated: "I've had one too many. I'm drunk."

Swales and Nelson drove on. They didn't know it at the time, but they had interrupted the killer in the act of raping and murdering Jane Dobson. Later, under questioning, the men were able to describe the appearance of the man they had seen for only an instant. They told the police that the killer wore a cap and leggings. His bicycle had the appearance of a racing bike with dropped handlebars.

Swales and Nelson drove on to the Dobson farm, unloaded some pigs, and returned past the area where they had seen the bicycle. It was now 5:45 p.m. The bicycle was gone and the men drove on, never giving the incident another thought.

Because the Hoolhouse family had been mentioned as the only ones Mr. Dobson could think of as enemies, police called on Robert Hoolhouse. They observed that he was pale, nervous, and had scratches on the right side of his face. Hoolhouse explained away the scratches and nervousness by telling the police that he had taken a rather bad spill off his bicycle. The police exchanged knowing glances when the bicycle proved to have dropped handlebars. Hoolhouse was taken to Haverton Hill police station where he gave a statement.

In essence he claimed that he had visited the home of William Husband on the day of Mrs. Dobson's murder. He called on Husband's daughter and a Miss Lax, remaining there until about 3:30 p.m. He stated that he left the Husband residence, which is located close to the Dobson farm, and cycled home, arriving at about 4 o'clock. It was on the trip home that he fell off his bike. That evening he returned by bus and accompanied Miss Lax to the movies at Billingham.

The story seemed plausible enough, and neatly removed Hoolhouse from the scene of the crime at 5:30, the most probable time of Mrs. Dobson's murder. Police hurried over to interview Miss Husband and Miss Lax. They corroborated Hoolhouse's story in every detail except one. They said that Hoolhouse didn't arrive until 3:45 p.m. and stayed for an hour and a half. That placed him squarely on the road at the crucial time with the opportunity to rape and kill Mrs. Dobson sometime after 5:15. Remember Swales and Nelson actually spoke to the killer at 5:30.

When the police returned to Hoolhouse and advised him

that Miss Husband and Miss Lax differed with his story as to times, he said that he must be mistaken. They were right. Poor Hoolhouse gave another statement, suggesting that he had made a terrible mistake the first time around.

Hoolhouse was arrested and charged with Mrs. Dobson's murder. The prosecution made much of the fact that Hoolhouse had fabricated fictitious times in order to place himself at his home at the time of Mrs. Dobson's murder. The scratches on his face weighed heavily against him. Hoolhouse's trial lasted three days. He was found guilty and sentenced to hang. All appeals failed, and he was duly executed at Durham Gaol.

Since Hoolhouse's execution there have been grave doubts expressed as to his guilt. Hoolhouse would not be the first innocent man to concoct a false story out of fear of being wrongly convicted.

Knowing that he was near the scene of the murder at the time it was committed, did Hoolhouse stupidly lie about the time to remove himself from the scene of the crime? The fact that he was in the vicinity at the time of the crime is not proof of guilt. Miss Lax swore that she hadn't noticed any scratches on Hoolhouse's face on their date at the movies. Did Hoolhouse have a legitimate fall off his bike the day after the murder when police noted the scratches? Knowing how incriminating they were, did Hoolhouse move his bicycle mishap up a day so that it would appear that he had the scratches before the murder?

We will never be certain of the answers to these questions. Hoolhouse never had the advantage of the real killer coming forward to confess all, as often happens in fiction. The truth of the Dobson case will forever remain a mystery.

THE PEASENHALL CASE

Years ago when young unwed women found themselves pregnant, their predicament was a source of more than a little embarrassment. In some instances their state became the catalyst that led to tragedy.

On this side of the Atlantic, the Chester Gillette case is considered the classic example. Chester's girlfriend informed him she was pregnant at precisely the same time that a rich socialite fell in love with him. Chester could see a life of wealth, power, and glamour slipping away. He killed the girlfriend and was executed for his trouble. The case was immortalized in Theodore Dreiser's best-selling book, *An American Tragedy.*

On the other side of the Atlantic the classic of all such involvements is known as the Peasenhall Case. The pregnant lady was Rose Harsent and the accused impregnator was William Gardiner.

It all began in 1902 in the tiny village of Peasenhall, which lies just north of Ipswich in Suffolk, England. Bill Gardiner was a respectable married man, having sired four happy, healthy children. The family lived in a pleasant enough cottage on Main St. Bill worked down the road at the only industry in the village, The Peasenhall Drill Works, which manufactured farm implements. He was a carpenter and held the position of foreman.

A big, dark, good-looking man, Bill's main activity outside his regular employment was his involvement with the church. He belonged to the Primitive Methodist Congregation and attended church regularly in the neighbouring village of Sibton. Actually, he did more than just attend. Bill was acting steward, treasurer, Sunday school superintendent, and, wouldn't you know it, choirmaster.

Because of these ecclesiastical pursuits, Bill was considered to be a pillar of the community. It is sad to relate, but often true, that the wives of men accused of impregnating sundry women are not themselves raving beauties. Mrs. Gardiner was a rather small woman, who for some reason seems to have developed a slight squint in both eyes. This distracting habit was coupled with an adolescent complexion, which never did clear up. Mrs. Gardiner was decidedly plain.

Rose Harsent was quite another story. She was a domestic servant at a rambling old gabled house known as Providence House in Peasenhall, which was the home of Deacon and Mrs. Crisp. Rose didn't run around, but there is evidence that indicates that the boredom of village life sometimes got the better of her. Rose had selected, discreet lovers.

Rose sang in the choir and it was here that she became acquainted with Bill Gardiner. Each evening after practice the choirmaster gave Rose a lift home to Peasenhall from Sibton.

Village life being what it was in those days, it was only natural that rumours began to spread about Rose and Bill. There were those who said that each evening the choirmaster taught Rose more than singing. The vague rumours came to a head when two boys named Skinner and Wright openly said that they followed Bill and Rose into a vacant thatched building referred to by the locals as the Doctor's Chapel.

The religious mores of the church couldn't ignore such an accusation. An inquiry was held under the direction of Mr. John Guy, a big wheel down at the church. The two boys stated that they had sneaked up within listening distance of Bill and Rose and had heard them giggling, and get this, they heard Rose say, "Oh, oh."

Both Bill and Rose denied any such meeting, claiming the story was made up by the two lads. The church investigation cleared the accused couple of wrongdoing.

We will never know what went on between Bill and Rose before the church inquiry. We will also never know if anything transpired between the two after the inquiry. But we do know that in May 1902, Rose was six months pregnant.

On May 31 there was a violent thunderstorm over Peasenhall. Heavy rains fell for hours. It was indeed a portentous night.

At 10 p.m. Mrs. Crisp said goodnight to Rose and retired for the night. Later, Mrs. Crisp, sleeping fitfully due to the thunder, thought she heard a dull thud coming from Rose's room. Her husband convinced her it was just the storm and she ignored the strange noise. The storm abated at 4 in the morning and the villagers slept peacefully thereafter.

Next morning Rose's brother, William Harsent, went to Providence House to deliver some clean linen to his sister. He had the distressing experience of finding his sister's body in a pool of blood at the foot of a stairway. Rose had been stabbed in the breast and her throat had been twice slashed from ear to ear. The body was dressed only in a nightgown and stockings. The lower portion of Rose's nightdress was burned, as were her legs. Beside the dead girl was a broken lamp. The body lay on a copy of The East Anglian *Daily Times.*

No weapon was found at the scene, but a broken bottle that had contained paraffin was lying close to the girl's head. The label on the broken bottle contained the words "Two to three teaspoons, a sixth part to be taken every four hours – Mrs. Gardiner's children."

Investigating officers gained a wealth of clues, all pointing to one man. The broken bottle, which had obviously been in the Gardiner home at one time, was strong evidence, but there was more. Rose's brother not only delivered fresh linen, he swore he had delivered the newspaper found under his sister's body to William Gardiner a few days before the murder. Then there was a gameskeeper named James Morris who was up and about at the moment Rose's body was discovered. He was aware of the scandal involving Bill Gardiner and Rose. This young sleuth found footprints leading from Gardiner's house to Providence House and described the pattern made by the rubber-soled shoes. Bill Gardiner had a pair of shoes with exactly the same pattern.

A letter was found in Rose's room: "Dear R, I will try to see you tonight at 12 o'clock at your Place if you Put a light in your window at ten o'clock for about ten minutes. Then you can take it out again. Don't have a light in your Room at twelve as I will come around to the back."

It was established that Bill Gardiner had the unusual habit of capitalizing the first letter of words in the middle of sentences.

On June 3, three days after the murder, Bill Gardiner, protesting his innocence, was arrested and charged with Rose Harsent's murder.

During Bill's trial the defence explained away most of the prosecution's case. Rose could have come into possession of Bill's newspaper in dozens of ways. Mrs. Gardiner swore that her husband was at home the entire night of the murder. Defence experts stated that the letter found in Rose's room could well have been written by someone other than Bill. Mrs. Gardiner explained how the incriminating medicine bottle found at the scene had come into Rose's possession. A few months prior to the murder, Mrs. Gardiner had a prescription filled for her children. The children had consumed the medicine and the empty bottle had remained in the family medicine chest. Later, Rose had come to her complaining of a sore throat. Mrs. Gardiner had taken some camphorated oil and placed it into the bottle with the incriminating label and given it to Rose. In this way the bottle had innocently come into Rose's possession.

Morris' evidence came under scathing cross examination. Was it natural for a man to memorize a footprint so that he could match it to a rubber-soled shoe from memory? The defence thought not.

Finally, as in so many other cases that have been argued before and since, there was not a drop of blood to be found on Bill Gardiner's clothes. Every stitch he owned was examined, but no bloodstains were ever found.

The jury retired to deliberate, but returned and advised the court that they were hopelessly deadlocked. A second trial was held in Jan. 1903. After deliberating for two hours and twelve minutes the foreman of the jury reported that they too were deadlocked. Bill was released from custody.

No other person has ever been tried for Rose's murder. While thunder roared and lightning flashed on the last day of May 1902, someone silenced her forever.

PART FIVE
BITS AND PIECES

THE BUTCHERED BRIDE

James Greenacre was a nasty man. He didn't go around killing people in wholesale lots, however. He was much more selective. James was a prosperous grocer who dabbled in local politics. He also manufactured and sold a terrific remedy, guaranteed to cure you of any ailment.

In 1835 he was a man who had almost everything. He lived comfortably in a large home in London, and had a wide circle of business and political acquaintances. The one thing he didn't have was a wife. There were plenty of young women around London at the time who would have been more than pleased to become Mrs. Greenacre. Unfortunately James insisted that they be well-endowed with cash, or property, or both.

In the meantime James did not live alone. His house-keeper, Sarah Gale, saw to it that his sex life was both active and stimulating. She even became pregnant and blessed James with a baby boy. The lad was a chunky four-year-old when James, continuing in his search for a rich wife, met Hannah Brown.

Hannah, who was fully aware of James' quest for a rich girl, let it drop that she had several parcels of choice property just waiting to be shared with the right man. James, at long last, thought his search was over. Hannah, however, was as poor as a church mouse. And Sarah did not take kindly to the idea of her man marrying Miss Brown.

As Christmas approached, Hannah told James that she thought the festive season was a good time to get married. She had one fear; that James would find out she was penniless and drop her. On the other hand, if she could get him to the altar in a hurry, she would reveal her destitute financial situation to him after the marriage. Hannah felt confident that all would be forgiven.

Hannah managed to get James to set the date of their marriage. It was to be on the last Wednesday of the year. They would have their very own intimate Christmas dinner at his house to seal the engagement.

Things were going along famously, but wouldn't you know it, some spoilsport told James that Hannah didn't have a penny to her name. She had actually been borrowing from her brother, based on the assumption that she would land Greenacre. James was fit to be tied. To think that he had come within an ace of being tied down to a woman whom he would have to support for the rest of her days.

It had been a close call for Sarah too. She knew that if James had gone through with the marriage her son would almost certainly be disinherited by his father. Now, she rubbed salt into James' wounds by telling him that if he declined to marry Hannah she would probably sue him for breach of promise. He would be held up to ridicule in front of his business and political acquaintances.

Sarah planted the seed of murder in James' mind. There was no alternative. The lying, deceiving Hannah wouldn't go away without raising an embarrassing fuss.

Christmas Eve came. Sarah answered the knock on the door. Radiant Hannah walked in and probably complimented Sarah on the beautiful banquet table. Greenacre entered the room. He couldn't restrain his anger. He verbally blasted Hannah, who admitted her lies and insinuated that now they were about to be married Greenacre was helpless to do anything about it. In a fit of anger, he picked up a rolling pin and with one vicious blow caved in his fiancée's skull. Hannah lay dead at his feet.

Sarah came up with a rather novel approach: "Let's cut her up into three pieces and deliver each one to a different district." If the three individual parts of Hannah were ever found, the authorities would think they had three mysteries on their hands and never connect the parts to one crime.

With his Sarah taking an active part, Greenacre managed to dissect the body. He delivered the head to Stepney and flung it into Regents Canal. The legs were disposed of in Coldharbour Lane, while the trunk, wrapped in a portion of a child's blue cotton dress, was dropped off in Kilburn.

Greenacre had a morbid Christmas, but things were looking up for a happy new year. He and Sarah were now indelibly bound together by the act of murder. They probably realized they were stuck with each other for the rest of their lives.

In the meantime, on Dec. 28, 1835, Hannah's torso was found in Kilburn. No one came forward to identify the torso, so it was preserved. Ten days later a lock keeper discovered the head in the Regents Canal. Despite Sarah and Greenacre's theory that no connection would be made between the two parts of the body, the Stepney police immediately contacted the Kilburn police. It was ascertained that the two parts were from the same body.

Hundreds of people viewed the body but it remained unidentified for a further two months. A basket maker found the parcel containing the legs in a ditch. The police now had the complete body.

Poor Hannah had only one living relative, her brother. He viewed the body and identified his sister. When questioned he said his last contact with his sister had been just before Christmas. She mentioned she was going to have Christmas dinner with James Greenacre. At that time he had inquired about his missing sister and had been told by Greenacre that the pair had quarrelled. Hannah had not shown up for dinner, and Greenacre said he never wanted to see her again.

The police turned their efforts towards our hero, James Greenacre. Neighbours told of hearing wild noises from the house on Christmas Eve. They all thought it strange that Sarah was cleaning and fumigating the house for days after Christmas. Most people clean up before the holiday, not after.

Greenacre heard of the questions being asked, and booked passage to the U.S. He was arrested only hours before he was to sail. A search of the Greenacre house produced the matching portion of the child's dress that had been used to wrap the torso.

Greenacre at first denied any knowledge of the murder. Then he said it was the result of an accident during the course of a practical joke. Finally he confessed to murder.

Both Greenacre and Sarah stood trial for murder in London's Old Bailey. Both were found guilty. Greenacre was publicly hanged before a jeering crowd of thousands on May 2, 1837. Sarah was sentenced to "transportation beyond the seas for life."

Sarah Gale eventually made a new life for herself in Australia. Fifty-one years later, in 1888, she died of natural causes.

HE CAME, HE SAW,
HE BURIED

The efficiency and cleanliness of the British, especially in the matter of murder, has never ceased to amaze me. The citizens of that tight little island are often careless and sloppy in other affairs, but absolutely never when it comes to murder.

At the turn of the century, young Edgar Edwards resided in Leyton. He was unemployed, with no prospects of changing that status. One day, while scanning the newspapers, he noticed a business for sale. We will never know whether it was at this moment that he decided to become a killer, or if he was studying the paper with the thought of murder already firm in his mind.

The business for sale was a grocery store owned by a Mr. Darby on Wyndham Rd., Camberwell. Edwards wrapped a heavy iron sash weight in newspapers and dashed over to Camberwell to take a look at the store. He arrived after business hours, and was let in by Mrs. Darby.

The grocery was a highly profitable venture for the Darbys. They explained that the only reason it was up for sale was because they had decided to move on to bigger and better things. In fact, because of the heavy trade during the Christmas season, they had to purchase a larger cashbox, and happened to have an unusual amount of cash on hand.

The Darbys, in their late twenties, appeared to have everything to live for, including a baby son. Edwards explained that he realized he was inconveniencing them, but he was a busy man himself and would appreciate taking a look at the books. Mrs. Darby led Edwards into the living area, while Mr. Darby continued to work in the store proper. Edwards courteously held out a chair for Mrs. Darby, who sat down with her child on her lap. Then Edwards took out his sash weight and struck Mrs. Darby on the head with such force that the chair she was sitting on crumbled to the floor. The baby screamed. Edwards snuffed out the child's life with two quick blows of the sash weight. Mr. Darby, hearing the commotion, rushed into the room. The sash weight came down on his head again and again. The three Darbys lay still in death on their living room floor.

Edwards didn't grab the cashbox and run. He had other plans. He coolly and callously dismembered his three victims and placed their bodies in three separate packing cases. He packed the contents tight with the addition of straw. He was in a grocery store, so there was an abundance of packing material available. Into a fourth crate Edwards tossed the sash weight, chair, and rug from the murder room. All four boxes were secured with nails and cord. Edwards, using the Darbys' typewriter, typed a note to the effect that they had sold their business, which would soon reopen under new management. He tacked the note on the front door. Edgar Edwards washed up and went home.

The next morning Edwards, using the Darby's money he had taken from the cashbox, rented an attractive house on Church Rd., Leyton. The rest of his rather hectic day was spent systematically removing everything of value from the Darbys' living quarters. Edwards had rented a truck and hired two local lads to help him with the heavier pieces. He took particular care of four securely wrapped packing cases.

Many of the Darbys' regular customers who came to shop at the store were shocked to read the notice on the front door. Edwards met them and was quick to point out that while the sale of the business appeared to be very hasty, it really wasn't so. He had been negotiating with the Darbys for weeks. They had come to terms only the evening before. The Darbys had dashed away that very same evening in order to close a deal they had been working on in Northern England. The story had the ring of truth to it. The Darbys had mentioned to many of their customers that they were trying to purchase a larger business. No one was even mildly suspicious.

Edwards spent one whole night digging in his back yard. He dug a large hole and placed the three Darbys and the box of incriminating furniture inside. Out of sight, out of mind. He had apparently succeeded in getting away with murder.

For a time all went well. Edwards spent most of his evenings at home, reading. His daylight hours were often spent in the library. Edwards neither drank nor smoked. He made the acquaintance of a young, respectable woman, who soon became infatuated with her polite, mild-mannered suitor. The pair became engaged. The only worry that Edwards had during these months was the ever-diminishing number of pound notes in the Darbys' cashbox.

Back at the Darbys' store the police had run into a blank wall. They deduced that the Darbys had absconded with all their belongings and cash in order to avoid paying suppliers. The man who had moved the furniture no doubt was in league with the Darbys. They had no idea murder had taken place.

Edwards needed to refill his cashbox and logically decided that since everything had worked out so well the first time, he would try it all again. He picked a grocery shop that was up for sale. Edwards invited Mr. Garland, the owner of the shop, over to Church St. to discuss the deal. He had taken the precaution of purchasing a new sash weight to assist in the negotiations.

When Garland arrived, Edwards hit him over the head with the sash weight. Instead of caving in, Garland screamed and fought his attacker. His screams brought the assistance of neighbours, and the struggle came to an end.

When the police arrived, Edwards was in bed, claiming that Garland must be crazy. He stated that Garland had attacked him for no apparent reason. Edwards said that he was sorry if Garland had his head split open in the struggle, but he was only acting in self-defence. The sham didn't work.

During the fight a desk had overturned. Stationery bearing the Darbys' name had scattered across the floor. Once the police found something connecting Edwards with the missing Darbys, they hung on like bulldogs. Friends and former customers of the Darbys were brought over to Church St. They recognized pieces of furniture as belonging to the missing couple. The police then came up with the two lads who had helped move the four sealed crates. They identified Edwards as the man who had hired them. The police discovered newly turned earth in the back yard. They dug up the bodies of the three Darbys.

Edwards stood trial for murder. He never confessed, and in fact refused to discuss any relevant aspects of his case. During the proceedings he often confided to his lawyer that the whole thing was a lot of nonsense and was an utter bore.

He was found guilty and sentenced to be put to death. As his execution date approached he became more cheerful and talkative. Edwards joked and laughed on the scaffold before the trap door was sprung.

A GRISLY FIND

It is one thing to want to live in a certain city. It is quite another thing to lose one's head over it. Santosh Kumari Bali did just that. This tale of terror begins in New Delhi, India, and ends in Toronto, where Mrs. Bali did, in fact, lose her head.

Mrs. Bali, a forty-two-year-old divorcée, made her living in New Delhi in the real estate game. When Harbhajan Singh Math, thirty-six, told her of the opportunities that existed in Canada, she could hardly wait to leave India. There were a few minor problems, but nothing seemed to be too difficult for Harbhajan to handle. He arranged for airline tickets, passports, and took care of other immigration red tape. Mrs. Bali travelled to the promised land in July 1974.

After her arrival things just didn't work out. As soon as her 30-day visitors' permit ran out she was told by Harbhajan that she was now an illegal immigrant, which was true enough. She could obtain employment only where details such as social security numbers and unemployment insurance deductions could be passed over. Leave it to Harbhajan to fix things. It so happened his brother Harmohinder Singh Math, thirty-four, and the latter's wife, Paranjit Kaur Math, twenty-eight, would be only too glad to assist Santosh in getting a job as a domestic. With Paranjit's assistance, Santosh was employed as a domestic in the home of Mr. and Mrs. André Allain of Weatherstone Cr. in North York, a suburb of Toronto.

Later evidence indicated that Harbhajan threatened to reveal Santosh's illegal status unless she turned money over to him. Terrified of being exposed as an illegal immigrant, Santosh paid off Harbhajan each month. Finally, after being blackmailed for almost a year, she informed Harbhajan that she would pay no longer.

That's where things stood with Santosh and the Math clan until Sept. 1975. On Sept. 15, two garbage collectors in Etobicoke were startled to discover that the trash can at the corner of Bloor St. W. and Eagle Ave. contained more than trash. They uncovered a female torso wrapped in burlap. On the very same day the Allains reported Santosh Kumari Bali missing. Two days later a woman's left leg was found sticking out of a pail beside a North York factory.

After questioning the Allains, police suspected that the torso and leg might be those of the missing woman. Upon searching Santosh's room, they found the addresses and telephone numbers of the Maths. As a result, Staff Sgt. Murray Crawford ended up at the Math residence on Burnett Ave.

Harbhajan admitted knowing Santosh slightly. He claimed that she was away on a trip to Montreal. A search of the Math residence revealed pails, plastic bags, and burlap sacks that matched material used to wrap the torso and leg. At Harmohinder's home on Steeles Ave., police found Santosh's coat, which Mrs. Math claimed belonged to her.

All three Maths were arrested and charged with murder. Because of the illegal status of the victim, and the lack of identification due to the missing head, it became imperative to legally identify the body as that of Santosh Bali. Two Toronto detectives, Staff Sgt. Gerald Stevenson and Sgt. Winston Weatherbee, flew to New Delhi to verify Mrs. Bali's identity. They brought with them X-rays and descriptions of operational scars found on the torso.

Weatherbee describes the trip as a strange but necessary one. "Mrs. Bali had a Caesarean section and a gall bladder operation some time before coming to Canada. We were able to confirm these facts with medical authorities and obtained other verification by interviewing members of Mrs. Bali's family."

In May 1976 the Maths stood trial for murder in a Toronto court. For thirteen days Crown Prosecutor Robert McGee built a formidable case against Harbhajan Singh Math. Math's brother and his wife remained silent, never admitting to any involvement in the case. There was very little connecting evidence McGee could bring forward against the couple, but Harbhajan was quite another kettle of fish.

Harbhajan claimed that Santosh had had a drinking bout in the basement of his home the previous Sept. 12. He said she had fallen on the concrete floor before passing out on a bed. Next morning when he attempted to wake her, she didn't stir. Santosh was dead. Harbhajan was in a fix. He knew that he would be in big trouble for assisting an illegal immigrant. Who knows, he might even be suspected of murdering Santosh. There was only one thing to do and that was to dispose of the body. Unfortunately, the rigid, unyielding corpse would not fit into his Volkswagen. Harbhajan thought for a moment, and then it all became clear. He would dismember the body and distribute the parts hither and yon.

In court, Math described his grisly task. "I started with a sickle, but it only got so far. It didn't work right, so I threw it away and picked up a saw. I cut the head off first." Calmly and unemotionally he described how some limbs were difficult and had to be twisted and pulled in order to be detached. He then took several trips in the Volkswagen to distribute the various parts of the body throughout the city. Above all, Math insisted that he did not murder Santosh.

Crown Prosecutor McGee remembers the Math case as "certainly my most gruesome case in fourteen years as a Crown Prosecutor." He recalls Math using a Bible to illustrate how he wrapped portions of the body. McGee felt certain that Santosh had been strangled, but without the head it was difficult to prove. The defence maintained that Santosh had met her death by falling several times on the concrete floor of his basement.

Defence attorney David Humphrey startled the court to stunned silence when he indicated that his client would reveal the location of the victim's head to the court. McGee describes the unusual manoeuvre as "the most amazing opening address I ever heard when the defence attorney suggested driving out to find the head."

It was obvious that the defence was trying to refute the Crown's contention that the victim had been strangled. And so the entourage of lawyers, doctors, and police found themselves being directed by the defendant to a field behind Holy Cross Cemetery north of Toronto. There, in the eerie darkness, in a plastic tote bag, the head of Santosh Kumari Bali was recovered.

Examination of the severed head proved that the defence was right all along. Santosh had not been strangled. However, this did the defendant little good, for he had made one fatal mistake. After cutting off Santosh's head he had thrown it in a pail containing engine oil. This coating of oil, along with the fact that the bag containing the head had lodged in nine inches of ice cold water all winter, combined to maintain the head in an excellent state of preservation.

Dr. John Ferris, a pathologist, indicated that the cause of death was asphyxiation. The victim's jaw was fractured in two places. Santosh had been beaten to death. Her nose was broken, her eyes blackened, and her head badly bruised and lacerated.

One minor mystery remains unsolved to this day. No blood was ever found on the pails, saw, and sickle Harbhajan professed were used during the dismemberment at his residence. It is the belief of investigating officers that Santosh was killed elsewhere. Her movements during her last hours on earth may never be known.

Due to the lack of evidence connecting Harmohinder

Math and his wife, Paranjit, to the murder, the jury saw fit to find the pair not guilty. Harbhajan was not as fortunate. He was found guilty and received the severest sentence possible at that time – life imprisonment with no possibility of parole for twenty years.

GOODNIGHT, IRENE

It takes no special talent to be a murderer. Ladies and gentlemen of a murderous bent come from all walks of life. They range from bungling morons to college professors. A select few take extraordinary steps to cover their tracks. As we have already seen, sometimes these steps include attempts to dispose of their victims' bodies.

Chester Stanton Jordan shifted his 225 lbs. from foot to foot as the clerk inquired if the hacksaw felt comfortable in his hand.

"Very fine," Chester replied. "It will do the job nicely."

The job Chester's nimble mind alluded to was the systematic dismemberment of his wife's body, but of course at the time only he knew that.

"I would appreciate it if you would sharpen the butcher knife."

"No problem at all," the obliging clerk responded.

Thus equipped with new cutting tools, the six-foot three-inch Chester ambled out of the hardware store to address himself to the task at hand.

As Chester smartly walked through the streets of Boston that day in 1908, the good citizens of Beantown had no way of knowing that Chester Jordan would soon be the best-known name in the city. Chester's cutting and hacking would provide the main news story for the Boston press for the following year.

Chester was born twenty-eight years earlier in Indianapolis. As a youngster he displayed a natural affinity for the stage, which prompted him to leave school to become an actor. To keep the wolf from the door, Chester supported himself by working between engagements in a furniture store. When he was twenty-one, his family moved to Boston. Chester developed an act and appeared on the stage whenever the opportunity presented itself.

In 1904 Chester met a stripper who disrobed under the name of Irene Shannon. It was considered politic for anyone appearing on the stage in Boston to have an Irish name.

On Sept. 25, 1904 Chester and Irene got married. They tried to combine their acting abilities by forming an act together, but their attempts were fruitless. Instead, Chester got a job as a collector for a finance company, while Irene was able to continue to make a living stripping.

It is difficult to say just when Irene began to accuse the hulking Chester of being impotent. Irene had the audacity to insinuate that Chester preferred male company to her own. Later, Chester claimed the whole topic of his impotence exploded into violence during an argument. He growled at his wife, "You're a dirty, evil-minded bitch" – to which Irene replied, "I'll show you whether I'm a bitch or not." Then the five-foot, two-inch Irene advanced on her huge husband with a butcher's knife. Chester, acting strictly in self-defence, you understand, struck his wife, sending her crashing down the stairs. Irene lay dead on the floor.

The next thing Chester remembers is waking up the following morning and finding his wife's nude body on the floor. Inexplicably, her throat was cut from ear to ear, but little details like that didn't seem to bother Chester.

What to do? Chester thought the whole thing over. If he went to the police he felt sure he would be accused of murdering his wife. Like many a murderer who went before him, Chester decided to dispose of the body.

He found a straight razor and a butcher knife in his home

and began his gruesome task. While the work wasn't easy, Chester managed to remove both arms and legs. He then lifted the armless and legless body and placed it in one of a pair of stationary stone washtubs. The arms and legs fitted nicely into the second tub.

Chester washed up and went to a neighbourhood bar, where he had a quick shot of whiskey to steady his nerves. He then visited the hardware store and purchased the hacksaw. At the same time he had the clerk sharpen his new butcher knife.

That evening Chester cut off Irene's head with his hack-saw. No one ever thought to ask so we will never know why Chester took the trouble to scalp his wife. We do know that he threw the scalp into the stove. The draft carried the scalp to the back of the stove, away from the flames. It was later recovered in almost mint condition.

Chester spent the entire evening cutting and carving until Irene was in a total of twelve individual sections. Exhausted and hungry, he paused to eat two cold pork chops. Ironically, they had been cooked by Irene the day before. Then Chester placed all twelve parts back into the two washtubs, cleaned up his tools, and left his residence to take a brief stroll.

Is a murderer's work ever done? When he returned from his walk, Chester placed Irene's head and thighs in the fur-nace. He lit the furnace and figured that was that.

Next day Chester bought a trunk and a spool of good strong cord. What remained of Irene he placed in the trunk. Chester went looking for a horse and wagon in which to transport his macabre cargo.

George W. Collins followed the honourable profession of what was then called a hackman. He was hailed by Chester and for the rest of his life was able to tell cronies the story of how he lugged Irene Shannon's body through the streets of Boston.

Earlier in the day Chester had rented a room at #7 Han-cock St. from a Mrs. Mary Haley. He gave the landlady four dollars for the first week's rent.

Collins, who wasn't a big man, had some difficulty placing

121

the trunk on his hack, but his obliging fare gave him a hand. Collins couldn't help but notice that his passenger drew the shades of the hack even though it was broad daylight.

Finally the horse-drawn vehicle pulled up in front of #7 Hancock. Again Collins' passenger helped carry the heavy trunk. The men lugged the trunk up the stairs and placed it in what was obviously Chester's room. Collins received a dollar for his trouble and took his leave, but he couldn't get the big man and the strange trunk out of his mind. He went to the police and told his story.

The police didn't think the incident was extraordinary, but they promised to look into the matter. That evening two police officers intercepted Chester as he was returning to his room. They asked him what was in the trunk. Chester hedged. Under further probing, Chester opened the trunk and began to lift clothing from a tray inset in the top of the trunk. One of the policemen became impatient. He lifted the tray and peered inside. Sure as shooting, Irene was in the trunk.

Chester was hustled down to the police station, where he confessed to dismembering his wife in an attempt to dispose of the body. He certainly hadn't murdered dear Irene. It had all been a horrible accident.

It took the Boston cops exactly one hour to formally charge Chester with murder. It took only three more hours for those same cops to find out that Chester had a well-heeled brother-in-law, none other than Jesse Livermore.

In 1908 Livermore's name was synonymous with American success stories. Jesse had left school at fifteen to work for a brokerage house in Boston. Starting with $3.12 he netted $140 on his first deal in the stockmarket. On the way up Jesse married a secretary who worked at another brokerage office. The secretary, Nettie Jordan, was none other than our boy Chester's sister. Within a year Nettie and Jesse Livermore had made their first fortune trading in copper stocks. Moving on to Wall St., they cleaned up over $3 million in cotton. No question about it, Chester had wealthy champions in his sister and brother-in-law. They publicly stated they would stand behind Chester, no matter what.

Chester stood trial for murder on April 20, 1909, in East Cambridge, Mass. He stuck to his story throughout, but the prosecution's evidence proved positively embarrassing. An efficient medical expert testified that Irene had not met her end by falling downstairs. She had died from manual strangulation.

The police had found a flatiron in Chester's residence. A medical expert, displaying poor Irene's skull in court, neatly fitted the flatiron into depressions in the skull. From the evidence it appeared impossible for Irene to have met her death by falling down the stairs.

Twenty hours after retiring to deliberate, the jury found Chester guilty as charged. With Livermore's bankroll behind him, Chester was able to exhaust every possible legal avenue in order to stay out of Massachusett's dreaded electric chair.

It was all for naught. On Sept. 24, 1912, Chester was firmly strapped into the electric chair. One minute and eight seconds later Chester was pronounced dead.

PATRICK WAS A
CHARMER

Whatever else I might say about Patrick Mahon, I have to admit he was a handsome devil. Not only was Pat's countenance pleasing to the eye, he also had a charming manner and was fastidious about his personal appearance. All in all, a fine cut of a man.

In 1923 Pat had already been married for thirteen years, having wed a remarkable young woman who was to stand by him through good times and bad. There were a few rough spots in Pat's past, but nothing compared to those that were to come.

For example, there was the time shortly after his marriage when Pat forged a cheque and took off to the Isle of Man with another woman. This little escapade landed him in jail for twelve months. Of a more serious nature, in 1916 he broke into a bank. During this robbery he struck a female employee over the head with a hammer. Pat spent five years in prison for that caper.

Throughout these exploits Mrs. Mahon stuck by her man. She gave birth to two children, a son and a daughter. The son died while Pat was serving his prison term.

To support her family while Pat was in prison, Mrs. Mahon took a job in London with the Consols Automatic Aerators Co. as a clerk. Ambitious and hard-working, she received several promotions, and advanced to a responsible secretarial position.

Through her influence she secured a job for Pat with her firm when he was released from prison. He too, proved to be somewhat of a success, and climbed quickly from salesman to sales manager.

All things considered, the Mahons were making something of their lives. Except for one thing. Pat couldn't stay away from women. With his charm and good looks he could have the pick of the crop.

By 1923 Pat was entwined in a prolonged affair with shorthand typist Emily Kaye. Emily worked for a firm of chartered accountants who had business dealings with Pat's company. Emily, who was thirty-seven, was completely enamoured of her handsome boyfriend, who was four years her junior. As the affair wore on, Pat vaguely hinted that someday he would leave his wife and be free to marry his very willing mistress.

Emily became disenchanted with vague promises. She sported an engagement ring and told acquaintances that she and Pat were planning to marry and move to South Africa, where Pat had an executive position waiting for him. Emily, who had been working steadily for twenty years, had a tidy nest egg of several hundred pounds stashed away.

In anticipation of Pat's divorce and her own marriage, she quit her job. Her income was now being augmented by the investments Pat made with her money. Every so often he borrowed a hundred pounds, with the promise of substantial profits in the future.

At this time Pat was going along with the tide, delaying love-struck Emily with plausible excuses – difficulty in obtaining passports, trouble with his wife. He hoped to keep Emily on the string forever. Meanwhile, he was blowing her hard-earned savings at the racetrack.

This idyllic situation received an abrupt jolt one day when Emily informed Pat that she was pregnant. Pat gulped. To alleviate any fears Pat might have about their future together,

Emily suggested they go away for a few days as a sort of love experiment. Not to a sleazy room, but to a real home. It would prove that they were meant for each other and could live happily ever after. Pat, who was always game for anything, thought it was a great idea.

Emily had another firm hold on Pat. One day, quite by coincidence, Emily was cleaning out a drawer which was lined with old newspapers. There, staring up at her, was an account of Pat's trial concerning the bank holdup and his five-year prison term. Emily knew that Pat dearly loved his position as sales manager. If exposed as an ex-convict to his employer he would most certainly be dismissed. In her subtle way Emily let Pat know that she wouldn't be above such a ploy if deserted. No wonder Pat opted for the love experiment.

Pat chose for his romantic interlude a desolate stretch of beach situated between Eastbourne and Wallsend on Pevensey Bay. This two-mile strip of Sussex beach is commonly referred to as the Crumbles. Located on the Crumbles were some cottages, which were once part of the Langley Coastguard Station. Early in April 1924 Pat rented one of the isolated cottages, using the fictitious names of Mr. and Mrs. Waller. He paid for the first week's rent in advance.

The month of April proved to be a very busy one for Pat. Let's follow his movements step by step. On Monday, April 7, Emily travelled to Eastbourne and checked into a hotel. On Thurs., April 10, Pat, still in London, met young, attractive Ethel Duncan on the street. It was raining. Pat offered to share his umbrella and walked Miss Duncan home. Charming, attentive, and polite, Pat had no difficulty obtaining a dinner date with Miss Duncan for the following Wednesday.

On Fri., April 11, Pat joined Emily in Eastbourne and took possession of their cottage on the Crumbles. Pat didn't stay the night, but returned to London.

On Sat., April 12, Pat returned to Emily at the cottage for the weekend. On Tues., April 15, Pat murdered Emily Kaye. On Wed., April 16, Pat travelled to London, purchased a butcher knife, then kept his dinner date with Miss Duncan.

During their dinner date, Pat invited the thoroughly enthralled Miss Duncan to spend the following weekend at his cottage by the sea. Miss Duncan was lonely. She had recently lost her job. Her handsome companion, who quoted Latin phrases and spoke French fluently, was very debonair. She accepted the invitation. Later, the thoughtful Pat sent her four pounds to cover the expenses for her trip.

And so Miss Duncan travelled to the lonely Crumbles to spend her weekend of love with her charming stranger. The cottage may have been thought by some to be drab. Others might have called it rustic. Miss Duncan loved the location. She loved the cottage and, above all, she loved Pat Mahon.

The attractive couple made love whenever the mood came upon them. Sometimes, spent from their efforts, they cuddled in silence, staring into the fireplace. Who knows, thought Miss Duncan, someday Pat might be divorced from his horrible wife and be free to marry me. He was so kind, so gentle. It was perfect with him, like being married. She had the run of the cottage. All except one room, which was always locked.

Miss Duncan had no way of knowing she was making love to a monster, while the body of Emily Kaye lay in the locked room awaiting the very special machinations of Patrick Herman Mahon.

Ethel Duncan left the Crumbles with a kiss and a promise of future love trysts. Later Pat was to state that he needed to have someone around for company after Emily's death. Unfortunately for Miss Duncan, she happened to be that someone.

While Pat had been busy spending time with his two lady friends, back in London, his wife became suspicious of his long absences.

It was true his occupation as sales manager necessitated a certain amount of travel, but lately he had spent every weekend, as well as several weekdays, on the road. When questioned, Pat always seemed to have an answer. However, when a friend mentioned that he had seen Pat at Plumpton Races Easter Monday, it was just too much. Mrs. Mahon felt Pat had slipped back to heavy gambling. She decided to search his suits for any evidence that he had been attending the races.

As she was looking through his pockets, Mrs. Mahon came across a cloakroom ticket from Waterloo Station. She was puzzled. What would her husband leave on deposit in a cloakroom? She decided to ask a friend, who by coincidence had once worked as a railroad policeman, to investigate the matter for her.

This gentleman presented the ticket at Waterloo and withdrew a Gladstone bag. He peeked inside and immediately called Scotland Yard.

Detectives put a guard on the cloakroom and returned the ticket to Mrs. Mahon with instructions to put it back in Pat's suit. The distraught woman asked what was going on, but could only find out that the ticket had nothing to do with bookmaking, which up to this point was Mrs. Mahon's greatest fear.

Next day, Pat Mahon strolled up to the cloakroom and claimed his Gladstone bag. Detectives picked him up without any fuss. He was taken to Kennington Road Police Station and asked to explain the contents of the Gladstone.

It had contained a large butcher knife, bloodstained clothing, and a tennis racquet case monogrammed E.B.K. All of these items had been liberally sprinkled with disinfectant.

Initially Pat attempted to dream up some story about transporting dog meat, but this tale quickly crumbled when he was informed by the police that tests had already been done on the bloodstained clothing. The blood was human.

Pat then confessed, but his confession was riddled with lies in an effort to cover up one of the most ruthless premeditated murders ever committed. According to Pat, he and Emily had an argument that ended up in a struggle. They fell to the floor with him on top. Emily struck her head on a coal scuttle, which killed her instantly. He then moved her body to a spare room, locked the door, and proceeded to have his new guest, Miss Duncan, down to the Crumbles for a pleasant weekend interlude.

When Miss Duncan left, Pat told police he cut the body into small pieces in an attempt to rid himself of the ghastly thing.

Detectives, accompanied by a pathologist, proceeded to the cottage on the Crumbles. They opened the front door and walked into hell. Throughout the cottage was the grim evidence that a human being had been methodically sliced and carved into small pieces. There was no doubt that the unfortunate victim was Emily Kaye.

Bloodied articles of female clothing were found in a trunk with the initials E.B.K. painted on its top. Four large portions of a human body were in the trunk. Greasy saucepans were scattered throughout the cottage. Upon examination the grease proved to be human fat. One two-gallon pot contained a piece of boiled human flesh.

Other human remains were found. Thirty-seven small pieces of human flesh were taken from a hat box, while a biscuit tin concealed human organs. Detectives also uncovered a bloodied rusty saw. Ashes from a fireplace contained bits of charred bone. A broken axe was believed to be the murder weapon.

Detectives and the pathologist gathered up the bits and pieces of what had once been Emily Kaye and returned to London. Little by little they reconstructed the body as best they could. The head and one leg were never found.

Pat Mahon was arrested and stood trial for the murder of Emily Kaye. Pat tried to turn on the charm that he had used to his advantage all his life. This time it didn't work.

He took the stand in his own defence and explained that Emily had struck her head on the coal scuttle, causing instant death. He also claimed that he had purchased the butcher knife after Emily's death, indicating that the dismemberment was not planned.

However, the prosecution was quick to point out that the quality of the coal scuttle was so poor that falling on it would scarcely cause a fatality. The prosecution also proved by receipts that Pat had purchased the butcher knife on the morning of April 12, when Emily was still alive. It was obvious to the jury that he knew what he was about to do and knew exactly how he would do it.

Pat readily admitted dismembering the body. His main hope was to attempt to discredit premeditation and attribute the death to an accident.

The courtroom was silent as Pat related how, on a stormy day, he built a roaring fire in the fireplace and positioned his victim's severed head on a log. As the flames leaped about the grisly object, Emily's eyes suddenly popped open. At that exact moment there was a flash of lightning and a clap of thunder. Pat, frightened out of his boots, ran out the door. It was some time before he could re-enter the cottage of death. Doctors explained that exposure to heat could cause the eyelids of a severed head to open.

Three days later Pat was still on the witness stand going through his gory tale step by step. Again he approached the part of the story that concerned the burning of the head. Suddenly, a thunderclap shook the courtroom. Many spectators gasped. Pat, visibly shaken, steadied himself on the witness railing.

Pat claimed that he had completely burned the head, but no trace of any part of it was found in the ashes of the fireplace. Scotland Yard believed that he burned what he could and possibly pulverized the balance into powder, which he threw into the sea.

Patrick Mahon was found guilty and sentenced to be hanged. All appeals failed to save his life. He was hanged on Sept. 9, 1924 at Wandsworth Prison.

PART SIX
CANADIANS

DEATH ON
CENTRE ISLAND

Bill Newell was a ladies' man. Good-looking, muscular, oozing confidence. Born in Toronto on May 20, 1914, Bill led an ordinary early life. His most outstanding accomplishment appears to have been in athletics. He was pole vault champion of Scarborough Collegiate Institute.

Bill married Winnifred Moores in 1934. He and Winnifred had a daughter, Doreen, but the marriage didn't last. A year before his divorce he was living with attractive Aune Paavola, the daughter of strict Finnish immigrants. Three weeks after his divorce from Winnifred became final, Bill married Aune, who had given birth to his son, Bill Jr., some six months previously.

Aune Paavola accepted Bill at face value. It was true his charming manner was often interspersed with impulsive temper tantrums, but she tried to overlook such minor faults.

However, Aune eventually became disenchanted with Bill's uncontrollable temper and his wandering ways. The couple separated. Bill rebounded without missing a bounce. Within a year he was living with another Finnish Canadian girl, Elna Lehto.

It was 1940. Russia had invaded Finland. In a grandiose gesture, Bill joined a Canadian force going to Finland's aid. Two months later, on April 5, he was back in Toronto. It was an embarrassingly short tour of duty, but Bill came up with a plausible explanation. He claimed that he had received serious wounds around one eye, forcing him to return to Canada.

As usual, Bill was lying. It was later learned that he had refused to sign an agreement to serve with the Finnish forces. As a result, he was deported to Canada. So much for Bill Newell's distinguished two-month war record in defence of Finland.

On Aug. 26 Bill joined the R.C.A.F. and was sent to Brandon, Manitoba for training. For the first time in years Bill had a steady income. It was the distribution of his Air Force dependents' allowance cheques that gave rise to his problems.

Aune was still Bill's legal wife. She and her son Billy were certainly entitled to some kind of living allowance. Then there was Winnifred, who had the full responsibility of raising Doreen. Also squarely in the picture was Bill's current companion, Elna, who, according to the Canadian Armed Forces, could not claim common-law status as she and Bill had not been living together for a full year. The only way Elna could share Bill's income would be if Aune signed an agreement to that effect or consented to a divorce.

Using his muddled affairs as an excuse, Bill obtained a transfer from Brandon to St. Thomas, Ont. On Sept. 20, 1940 he returned to Toronto on leave and spent almost every evening with Aune.

Bill made arrangements. On Sat., Sept. 28, he spent the night with Aune. He planned to take her and her roommate, Orvokki Hakamies, to a concert at the Active Service Canteen. At 8 a.m. he left Aune and returned to Elna, but stayed only a few hours. At noon he took Aune out to lunch, telling Orvokki that they would return in an hour or so.

When they left Aune's home at 15 Grange St. at 1:30 that Sunday afternoon, there is little doubt that Bill Newell was leading his wife to her death.

Mrs. Toini Ranpors, the girls' landlady, thought Bill

looked gallant in his crisp new Air Force uniform. She watched the good-looking couple as they walked east on Grange and turned south on Beverley. They had a bite to eat at the Active Service Canteen about 2 p.m., walked down to the ferry docks and caught the 2:50 boat, the Sam McBride, to Centre Island.

They strolled hand in hand down Manitou and Iroquois Avenues onto a footpath to the northeast section of a filtration plant located there. They were within a stone's throw of St. Andrew's Cut, one of several lagoons intersecting the island's coast. It was an isolated, lonely place.

Aune had believed that there was still hope for a reconciliation with her husband, but now she knew it was no use. Bill was pressing for a divorce or, failing that, was attempting to have her sign off her rights to his family allowance cheques. Aune would have none of it.

Suddenly Bill pounced on his wife. Aune struggled. A rope was twisted around the hapless girl's neck and pulled until she lay dead. All was quiet in that isolated, overgrown section of Centre Island. Bill's mind raced with the details of what still had to be done.

Without warning, unexpected intruders came upon the scene. Charles and Marion Maynes, who lived on the island, were canoeing through St. Andrew's Cut. Bill saw them first. He propped Aune's body up to a sitting position, tied a string on a stick and pretended to be fishing. Mrs. Maynes later testified that she thought it strange that the woman sitting so erect seemed to be staring straight ahead. She noticed the airman fishing and looked away.

Slowly the Maynes disappeared from view. Bill carried his wife's body off the path and stripped it of everything that might identify her. He covered Aune's body with her black coat. Then he gathered as much brush as he could find and dumped it over her inert form. With luck, Bill thought, the body might not be found until spring.

Bill caught the 4:30 ferry back to the mainland. At 8:45 he met Orvokki Hakamies and inquired if Aune was at home.

134

When Orvokki replied that she didn't know where Aune was, Bill continued on to his living quarters with Elna at 172 Howland Ave.

Aune Newell was immediately reported missing. Next day Bill returned to St. Thomas. On Tuesday, in an attempt to allay suspicion, he wrote a pleasant letter to Aune.

Bill managed a 48-hour leave. This time Elna met him with the disconcerting news that there were radio reports of his wife's disappearance. She suggested that he contact police. Bill took the advice and told Detective Sgt. Fred Skinner that, in his opinion, his wife was not missing, but hiding somewhere to avoid being served with divorce papers. He also told Skinner that he had last seen his wife the previous Sunday at 7 p.m., when he had bumped into her at the corner of Yonge and Adelaide Streets.

On Sun., Oct. 6, Harry Lemon, a parks department employee, whose job it was to make a circuit of Centre Island every Sunday, spotted a woman's shoe. It captured his attention because it appeared new. Harry looked further and found a garter, a purse, a stocking, and finally the body of Aune Newell. Exactly one week had elapsed since she had been strangled to death.

Bill was immediately picked up and held as a material witness while detectives gathered evidence. Bill's letters to Aune indicated that his main concern was to obtain a divorce and custody of his son Billy so that his service cheques could be diverted to Elna. A piece of rope was found at the scene. It matched rope found at 172 Howland Ave., where Bill lived with Elna.

Bill stood trial three times for the murder of his wife. The first two resulted in hung juries. He was an obstreperous prisoner, continually fighting with guards. During court proceedings he shouted at the presiding judge and witnesses.

New evidence was presented at the handsome airman's third trial. A torn Y.M.C.A. envelope with an R.C.A.F. crest had been found near Aune's body. The reassembled envelope revealed a sketch of the remote death site. Elna identified the map and notes as being in the handwriting of Bill Newell. He had written to her many times using similar envelopes. One was found among his belongings. Elna also testified that Bill had written her suggesting that the murder of his wife was the solution to his problems.

Bill Newell was found guilty and sentenced to hang. All appeals failed. On Feb. 12, 1942, Bill had a breakfast of bacon, eggs, toast, and coffee. He refused a sedative and, proclaiming his innocence to the end, walked erectly to the Don Jail scaffold, where he was executed.

BURIED ON THE FARM

"There was no direct evidence that murder had been committed, not even a body. Yet I knew that Viola had been murdered, and I had a pretty good idea who killed her. The case was bizarre in many ways," said Inspector Bill Perrin of the Ontario Provincial Police. Sitting in his office at the O.P.P. Headquarters talking about the apprehension of murderers, I got the distinct impression that once Bill Perrin becomes convinced of something he doesn't let go until he either proves or disproves his beliefs.

Inspector Perrin now operates out of the Anti-Rackets Branch, but for years was attached to the Criminal Investigation Branch, where he was in charge of many of Ontario's strange murder cases. None was stranger than that of Viola Leahy.

The Leahy farm is situated along R.R. #4, Lakefield, Ontario, and has been in the Leahy family for as long as anyone can remember; certainly four or five generations. Jim Leahy worked hard on the farm, and supplemented his income by operating heavy excavation equipment. Everyone agrees that Jim is one of the best operators in the Peterborough area. Viola, his wife of over twenty-five years, also had interests that drew her away from the farm. Before her marriage she had received formal training as a Registered Nursing Aide, a vocation she continued to follow after she became Mrs. Leahy. Both Jim and Viola had independent natures, and this independent bent, combined with their physical absence from each other, drove a wedge into an otherwise normal relationship.

Viola in particular craved some sort of social life. She enjoyed taking in the local dances, and sometimes visited a tavern with a woman friend, Emgard Woodzack, although she never drank anything stronger than a soft drink.

The long-standing marriage deteriorated until, finally, in 1972, Jim and Viola had an argument that turned into a fight. Viola charged her husband with assault. He was forced to appear in Family Court in Peterborough, where the charge was dropped. Viola then separated from Jim for a while and took legal action to obtain a half share of the family farm. For some reason known only to herself, she changed her mind and returned to live with Jim. Things were never the same after that. The Leahys settled down to a strange and unusual lifestyle. Viola supported herself. Jim did likewise. They conversed only when necessary. Viola continued to cook and wash Jim's clothing. They slept in separate rooms.

Every Friday, Viola would leave the farm and visit with Emgard. She always returned on Monday. And so, month after month, year after year, the strained lives of Viola and Jim Leahy continued.

Jim's brother Emmett worked a farm directly south of the Leahy farm. Actually, Jim had sold the house to Emmett some years before. Besides farming, Emmett had been steadily employed at the Westclox plant in Peterborough for the past twenty-five years. Emmett was raising four sons; the oldest, Ralph, was nineteen.

Although all was not well with the Leahy marriage, there was really nothing to distinguish them from hundreds of other farmers throughout the country: two brothers with adjoining farms, supplementing their incomes by working away from the soil. Hardly the scene for a bizarre and unusual murder.

In 1975 Jim suffered a fractured skull in a farm accident.

From that time on Emmett and his sons gave Jim a helping hand with the chores. Viola, too, was not well. She suffered from arterio-sclerosis (hardening of the arteries), which resulted in serious memory losses.

Because of the coolness between husband and wife, Viola came to depend a great deal on her brother and sister-in-law, Jack and Zetta Leeson. She phoned them every day. If she wanted to go anywhere, it was the Leesons who picked her up and brought her back to the farm.

On Fri., Sept. 17, 1976, Viola was picked up by Jack Leeson and taken to Peterborough, where she stayed with her friend Emgard. Two days later, on Sunday, Jim was admitted to Sunnybrook Hospital in Toronto to have bone chips removed from his skull. This confinement was the result of the fracture he had suffered two years previously. Thus Jim was away from the farm from Sept. 19 until his return from Sunnybrook on Oct. 3. He was never to see his wife again.

Meanwhile, Viola's movements are well documented. On Mon., Sept. 20th, she paid a visit to her doctor in Peterborough. The Leesons picked her up at her friend Emgard's, and gave her a lift to Dr. Flak's office. He prescribed pills and rest. Jack and Zetta Leeson then drove Viola back to the farm. They helped the sixty-five-year-old woman into the house with her luggage. They left the farm at about 7 p.m. It was the last time they ever saw Viola.

A half hour later Emgard received a phone call from her friend. The conversation was normal in every way. Viola gave no indication of unusual stress or anxiety. Emgard assumed that everything was fine.

Next day Zetta Leeson tried to reach Viola on the phone all day, with no success. On Wednesday Zetta and Jack drove over to the farm. They found Viola's luggage exactly where they had placed it the previous Monday. There were several cigarette butts in an ashtray. This bothered the Leesons, because they knew that neither Viola nor Jim smoked.

On Thursday they notified Emmett Leahy that Viola

could not be located. Together with Emmett, they searched the farmhouse but found nothing that could lead them to the missing woman. On Saturday, five days after she made the phone call to Emgard, Viola was reported missing by Jack and Zetta Leeson. The report was turned in to E.D. Martin of the Peterborough detachment of the O.P.P.

During the preliminary investigation into the missing persons' case the O.P.P. turned up three pieces of information that were later to prove of the utmost significance. David Ramsay had cleaned the furnace of the Leahy home on Sept. 22. The only person he had come in contact with on the property was young Ralph Leahy. Ramsay stated the boy seemed to be lurking near an open barn door when he spotted him. Ramsay was interested in getting someone to sign his bill that the work on the furnace had been completed. He thought it odd that when he approached Ralph with the bill the boy said, "I'm not supposed to be here." Ralph signed the bill.

Another bit of information that gave the investigators food for thought was Emmett Leahy's statement that although he was taking care of his missing sister-in-law's mail, it had disappeared from his house. Jack, Zetta, and Emmett remembered that when they searched the house on the 23rd of Sept., Ralph had mentioned that he had seen Viola at about 8 a.m. on Sept. 21. He thought she was heading for the bus.

The investigation continued. Jim Leahy came home on Oct. 3rd, into the midst of an investigation into his wife's disappearance. All of Viola's personal effects were found in the house. More and more it became apparent that she had met with foul play.

Two weeks went by. The Lakefield postmaster received an unusual piece of mail. It was a "Change of Address Notice," apparently signed by Viola Leahy, directing her mail to the Sudbury post office, General Delivery. The card was turned over to the O.P.P. They quickly established that the signature on the card was a forgery.

In the meantime Ralph left his father's farm to seek employment in Edmonton, Alberta. The police checked his handwriting against the signature on the Change of Address card and established that the signature had been forged by Ralph.

Detective Inspector A.D.R. Smith and Constable G. Katz thought that Viola Leahy had been murdered. Despite snide insinuations that she had taken off with a man, neither policeman believed it to be true. They flew to Edmonton to interrogate Ralph. At first he denied forging the signature. Then he admitted it, stating that a friend of Viola's had given him $50 to do it. Ralph was returned to Peterborough, and charged with uttering a forged document. On June 9, 1977, he received three months imprisonment, to be followed by a two-year probationary period.

On June 13, the then Detective Inspector Bill Perrin was assigned to the case. "I believed that Viola Leahy was dead," the Inspector says, "and that the case could only be solved through her nephew, Ralph Leahy." Perrin made the decision to place Constable Bill Campbell of the Intelligence Branch of the O.P.P. into jail with the suspect. Within a day Campbell was playing cards with Ralph in the Quinte Regional Detention Centre in Napanee. Other prisoners were preparing for a transfer to Kingston Penitentiary. Ralph told his new friend that he too would probably be transferred before he finished his current sentence. He bragged that he and a friend had killed someone during the course of a robbery. Campbell didn't press the matter, but made a date to get in touch with Ralph when both men were released.

On Aug. 9 Ralph Leahy was released. Unknown to him he was under constant surveillance by the O.P.P. The following night Campbell met with Ralph at the Jolly Roger Lounge of the Holiday Inn in Peterborough. During their conversation, Ralph boasted to the undercover agent that he had killed his aunt the evening after his Uncle Jim had gone to hospital in Toronto. Once Ralph began talking he wouldn't stop. He

141

confessed to seventeen or eighteen robberies, and bragged about serving two years in jail. Ralph thought he was impressing Campbell, who had posed as a member of an auto theft gang working between Montreal and Ontario. He wanted a job with the gang.

Campbell didn't believe any of Ralph's bragging, with one exception. He firmly believed he had a murderer on the line. They made a date to meet again on Aug. 13. This time Campbell brought along Constable Terry Hall, posing as his brother and fellow member of the auto theft gang.

Ralph was duly impressed. He talked incessantly of having killed his aunt. Late into the night the three men talked. In the end Ralph promised to show them where he had hidden Viola's body.

The following Friday the two officers and Ralph left the Holiday Inn at 1:30 a.m. for the Leahy farm. In deep bush beside a swamp, the three men dug for a body. Later, the officers were to relate that while Ralph dug he made derogatory remarks about his aunt. "You old bitch, where are you? You've given me enough trouble."

Throughout the early morning the men dug by flashlight, but Ralph couldn't find his victim's body. He promised his two friends that if they returned with him at some future date, he would produce the missing woman.

On Aug. 25, at 11:05 p.m., Inspector Perrin decided to pull the plug on the investigation. He arrested Ralph and, at the same time, picked up his girlfriend, Barbara Hartwick, for questioning. At the time Ralph remarked, "You'll never find her in a million years." When questioned, Barbara revealed that Ralph had admitted to her back in Nov. 1976 that he had killed his aunt. He said he had shot her three times.

Perrin interrogated the suspect. Ralph claimed he had nothing to say. Then he informed Perrin, "You made a mistake picking me up today, you should have waited a day and you would have had the body."

In the wee hours of Fri., Aug. 26th, Ralph indicated that he wanted to see Perrin. Perrin questioned and informed the suspect of his rights: "Are you prepared to show us where

Viola is buried? You know you don't have to show us or do anything that may be used as evidence, Ralph."

At the ungodly hour of 3:30 a.m., Ralph Leahy led the officers to the area beside the swamp where he and the two undercover agents had dug previously. He stated that he had marched his aunt down to the edge of the swamp, and had shot her three times with her husband's .22 calibre rifle. The murder weapon was turned over to Perrin.

Digging began later the same day, but try as they might, they couldn't find the body. Finally, Perrin brought in some heavy earth-moving equipment, and on Tues., Aug. 30, the shovel uncovered the body of Viola Leahy. She had been shot three times in the area of the chest and abdomen. Ballistic tests confirmed that two of the bullets had been fired from the Leahy's .22 rifle.

Later, Ralph told doctors that he hated his aunt. The killing had not been a spur of the moment sort of thing. He had mulled over the possibility of killing her for several weeks. After murdering his aunt at the edge of the swamp, he left her where she fell, but returned the next day with a shovel and buried her. He told the doctors that his aunt was not worth the time he was going to spend in prison. He had no remorse for what he had done and was only sorry that he would have to go to jail.

The rather smallish five-foot-six-inch farm boy had killed his aunt because he didn't like her. All indications are that she was kind and considerate to her nephew.

Viola Leahy had spent eleven months and ten days buried on her farm. On Feb. 4, 1977, her nephew, Ralph Leahy, was sentenced to life imprisonment. He will not be eligible for parole until he has served sixteen years of his sentence.

MURDER FOR PROFIT

Times were tough. The country was in the throes of the most disastrous depression this nation has ever known. None found it tougher than the isolated Canadian farmers who had no market for their produce. That's why William J. Larocque and Emmanuel Lavictoire decided to go into the murder business.

Both men owned scrub farms about a mile apart near L'Orignal, Ontario. No matter the amount of toil they expended, nothing seemed to lift them from the poverty they endured day by day. Both men were approaching sixty and had been close friends for years.

During the severe winter months, huddled beside their Quebec heater puffing away on their pipes, they plotted to insure the lives of acquaintances, murder them, and make the deaths appear to be terrible accidents. It is doubtful if Larocque and Lavictoire ever considered the possibility of being caught. They acted openly, with little regard for concealing their actions.

Athanase Lamarche was to be the diabolical pair's first victim. Athanase's father, Felix, was an elderly gentleman who resided in the township of Cumberland. Speaking as a friend of the family, Larocque approached Harvey Cameron, an agent for Manufacturer's Life Assurance Co. about insuring young Athanase. Cameron, ever on the lookout for

144

prospects, was pleased to set it up. Accompanied by Felix and Larocque, Athanase was issued a policy for $5,000, with double indemnity (providing for payment of twice the face value) in case of accidental death. Father Felix handed over the first premium of $62.50, a princely sum during the depression, and was promptly named beneficiary.

Athanase, who apparently was not all that swift, was then boarded out with a Mrs. Desjardins. This kind soul ran a home specializing in the care of the mentally afflicted. Not satisfied with the sum of $10,000 on Athanase's life, Larocque was successful in obtaining another $10,000 policy through Northern Life Assurance Co. Again Felix was named the beneficiary.

Athanase wasn't long for this world. On April 4, 1930, he accidentally fell off the ferry dock at Masson, Quebec, and promptly drowned. Chief witnesses to the unfortunate accident were none other than our friends Larocque and Lavictoire.

Daddy Felix collected from the insurance companies, but never seemed to be able to hold onto the loot. Larocque and Lavictoire only had to ask and Felix would cough up the amount requested. Lavictoire bought a new truck. Larocque picked up a sleek new Ford. It has been suggested that Felix was in on the plot to murder his own son, but in light of future events, this avenue of inquiry was never fully investigated. However, there seems little doubt that the two men were blackmailing Felix.

Everything had come up roses for the two friends now turned murderers. They looked around for additional victims. Insuring their prey proved to be more difficult than it had been with the unfortunate Athanase. Many applications were refused. For some reason, when they applied to La Société des Artisans Canadien Francais Insurance Co. for a $5,000 policy on Leo Bergeron's life, the application was accepted. When the policy was issued, it of course contained the double indemnity clause in case of accidental death. This time Larocque was named as beneficiary.

145

Leo Bergeron was a poverty stricken young farm labourer. It had been his misfortune to desperately need $10, and to have asked Larocque for some help. Larocque, never one to overlook an opportunity, hustled Leo down to the Bank of Nova Scotia in Rockland. The manager loaned Leo the ten spot and had Larocque sign a promissory note. In this way Leo was indebted to the cunning Larocque.

Leo, who laboured long and hard on the farm of Eugene Morin, began to smell a rat, or I should say rats. He had a premonition that Larocque and Lavictoire were planning to kill him.

During the harsh January of 1932, both Larocque and Lavictoire took turns trying to lure Leo over to Larocque's farm. Leo stubbornly refused to budge. He told Morin he knew that he would meet with foul play if he ever ventured onto Larocque's property. The two schemers persisted. They offered the young lad more money in one month than he could make in a full year working for Morin. Leo finally consented to visit Larocque at his farm. Lavictoire accompanied him.

Once there, Leo saw Larocque waiting for him beside a barn. A team of horses stood harnessed to a small portable thrashing mill. Leo walked into the barn. Larocque nonchalantly asked him to close a cowshed door. Leo complied.

When he turned around, the two men rushed him, jabbing him in the groin, hands, and arms with pitchforks. Leo ducked and weaved, screaming for mercy, but the men showed none. Using the handle of the pitchforks they rained blows upon Leo's head with such ferocity that one of the pitchforks snapped as the young man sank to the ground, his head a bloody mass. Larocque and Lavictoire then rushed the horses into the enclosed barn. Being whipped with no place to go, the team bucked and thrashed about, inflicting terrible blows with their hooves to Leo's prostrate form.

Larocque hid the pitchfork handle on top of a dusty old beam. According to a prearranged plan, Lavictoire dashed across a field to seek help in quieting the horses from a

146

neighbouring farmer, Alcide Deschamps. As Deschamps approached the barn he could hear the bucking horses and Larocque's obvious attempts to quiet them. With Deschamp's help, the men moved the portable threshing mill out of the barn and settled down the horses. There lay Leo Bergeron, with half his skull crushed away. Within an hour doctors and police were at the scene.

Police examined the horses' hooves. They were splattered with blood. It looked like a pure and simple farm accident. Before the body was removed, a police officer made a strange discovery. He found a broken pitchfork handle on a dusty beam. It was obvious that the handle had been recently placed there. Neither Larocque nor Lavictoire could explain the presence of the pitchfork handle. The handle wasn't perfectly clean. There were stains on it that were later identified as human blood. Blood stains were also evident on the walls, indicating that Bergeron must have received several blows that had bled profusely before he had fallen. Police wondered if any man could stand after being kicked repeatedly by two horses.

When the story of the two men's insurance schemes came to light, both men were arrested and charged with murder. Before going to trial the Crown had Leo Bergeron's body exhumed. Although an original post mortem had been conducted, indicating that Leo's injuries were consistent with being kicked to death by horses, this closer examination sealed the fate of the two accused men. Small puncture wounds were found in Leo's groin, arms, and hands. These were the wounds inflicted by the pitchforks, proving that Leo had been struck many times before the horses did their work.

Both men were found guilty of murder. On March 15, 1932, William Larocque and Emmanuel Lavictoire walked briskly to the scaffold built especially for the occasion in L'Orignal, and were hanged for their crimes.

WHO WAS HE?

If you drive along picturesque Highway #3 from Simcoe to Dunnville in southern Ontario, you will pass through the tiny hamlet of Nelles Corners. Just a few miles north of Lake Erie's shores, Nelles Corners is off the beaten track. In 1854 a crime took place in this community that gave rise to a series of events that made it one of the strangest murder cases in Canada's history.

John Nelles operated a general store. He and his wife lived together with his brother, Augustus, and his wife's sister, Lucy Humphreys. On the night of Oct. 18, the family had finished supper. The early evening was no different from hundreds that had preceded it. A chill wind whistled outside as one by one the family retired for the night. John, left alone at the kitchen table, took a long last pull on his pipe before knocking the ashes against the grate of the kitchen stove. He was about to go to bed when it happened.

Five men burst through the front door. Their intent was never in doubt. Their faces were blackened with burnt cork. The desperate men demanded money. Nelles rose from the kitchen chair, but made no attempt to comply with the robbers' wishes.

A shot echoed through the once peaceful home, and John Nelles sank to the floor. The badly wounded man moved slightly, eliciting a further shot from the pistol carried by one of the men. Mrs. Nelles and her sister Lucy rushed into the room and ran to John's aid. The five bandits tore a watch from the wounded man. Ignoring the women, they continued to search the house for anything of value.

Augustus Nelles woke up with the first shot. Wisely, he remained in bed; not the most heroic action, but one that most certainly saved his life. As quickly as the wanton killing had taken place, the five men opened the door and disappeared into the darkness.

A few miles down the road the killers bumped into two farmers, who were relieved of the few dollars they had in their possession. Within hours the unknown assailants had boarded a train bound for Buffalo. Once in the U.S. the men separated, having left heartache and tragedy in their wake.

Despite the fact that their faces had been blackened with burnt cork, a good description of the wanted men was given by the two women, as well as the two farmers who had been robbed. Three of the men, King, Blowes, and Bryson, were quickly apprehended. They were placed in prison in Cayuga, Ontario. All three men were tried, found guilty, and sentenced to death. King and Blowes were hanged, but Bryson's sentence was commuted to life imprisonment. He probably saved his skin by confessing to being one of the men in the house at the time of the murder. All three men claimed that they hadn't fired the fatal shot. They stated that the trigger had actually been pulled by one William Townsend.

Meanwhile, an event took place that had a direct bearing on the shooting at Nelles Corners. Approximately a month after the murder of John Nelles, two men entered a hotel operated by a Mrs. Jordan at Port Robinson, Ontario. While the two men were eating, other men in the hotel swore that one of the strangers looked like William Townsend, the wanted killer of John Nelles. They notified the authorities.

Several police rushed to the hotel to apprehend the wanted man. One of the policemen, Constable Charles Richards, faced the stranger, who immediately pulled a gun and shot him. The constable died a few hours later. The man known as Townsend got away.

Over two years went by, and again Townsend was recognized. This time he was taken into custody without incident by the Cleveland, Ohio authorities. The government of Canada immediately proceeded to have the wanted man extradited to Canada. In May 1857, he was delivered to the Canadian authorities and placed in jail in Cayuga to await his trial for the murder of John Nelles.

From the moment he was taken into custody, William Townsend captured the imagination of the country. Townsend remained hostile toward the authorities, but despite this hostility, well-placed powerful men took an interest in his case. Throughout his stay in custody and his ensuing trial, Townsend claimed that he wasn't Townsend at all. He swore he was Robert J. McHenry, a Scotsman who worked as a mariner out of Cleveland, Ohio. He further swore that he had been in California searching for gold at the time of John Nelles' murder.

Townsend's unusual trial began on Sept. 27, 1857. The Cayuga courthouse had never seen such an array of legal talent. The Crown was represented by Henry Smith, the Solicitor General of Canada. S.B. Freeman, Q.C., one of the finest orators of his time, represented Townsend. The accused pleaded not guilty. From the beginning the trial boiled down to the question of whether the accused man was Townsend or McHenry.

Lucy Humphreys identified the prisoner as the robber who had fired the shots that killed her brother-in-law. William Bryson was brought from Kingston Penitentiary to testify and identified the accused as the murderer Townsend. Sometime previous to the murder of Nelles, Townsend had been employed as a cooper in the neighbouring community of Dunnville. A number of former neighbours of the man in the dock took the stand, and all identified him as being William Townsend.

Surely this was enough to convict the prisoner, but such was not to be the case. Freeman paraded close to a hundred witnesses to the stand, all of whom swore that they knew Townsend well, and that the prisoner was not William Townsend. Townsend's brother-in-law, Ezra Smith, said the man in the dock was a stranger to him. Benjamin Diffin, who worked with Townsend one whole winter, said the accused was unknown to him. No expense was spared to place witnesses in the stand who swore the accused was not William Townsend.

After six hours of deliberation, the jury returned and informed the court that they were undecided. They were dismissed. The accused man was about to be returned to his cell when the deputy sheriff of Welland County read a warrant charging the prisoner with the murder of Constable Charles Richards of Port Robinson.

William Townsend, or whoever he was, was taken from Cayuga and lodged in the Welland (then called Merrittsville) Jail.

On March 26, 1858, he again stood trial for murder. Again his case rested on his claim that a terrible mistake had been made. He was not the murderer William Townsend. All the same witnesses were heard again. This time the foreman of the jury spoke out loud and clear, "The prisoner is McHenry, and is not guilty." That night the taverns of old Merrittsville rocked with celebrations held by McHenry's friends.

Townsend-McHenry was returned to Cayuga, for he still was in custody for the Nelles murder. But within a few days he heard that the Crown had no intention of trying him again. He was released on bail with the understanding that he would make himself available if the Crown ever decided to place him on trial again. This never happened. The strange, silent, hostile prisoner walked out of the Cayuga jail a free man.

For some time after, Robert McHenry was in great demand as a speaker at clubs and fairs throughout the country. Later, he dropped from sight and was never heard of again.

To some he was a killer named Townsend, who got away with murder. To others he was a harassed, innocent man named McHenry. Who was he? This question remains unanswered.

CANADA'S FIRST MURDER

Thomas D'Arcy McGee was born in 1825 in Carlingford, Ireland. At seventeen he heeded the adventurous call of the New World, making his way to Boston, where he obtained employment with a Catholic Irish newspaper, the Boston *Pilot*. By the time he was nineteen, he was editor of the paper.

The following year McGee returned to his homeland, and became an avid foe of Great Britain's union with Ireland. He was a leading figure in the Fenian Movement, an organization devoted to achieving Irish independence from England.

In 1848 McGee had to flee the country; some say he left disguised as a priest. He made his way once more to the U.S., but moved to Canada in 1857. A year later he was elected to the Legislative Assembly of Canada, representing Montreal West.

Once in Canada, it was assumed by Irish patriots that McGee would continue to expound his Fenian sympathies, but such was not the case. McGee split with the Fenians, believing their policy of violence too extreme. In fact, he became an adversary of the Fenian Brotherhood and was considered a traitor by many sympathizers of that movement.

On the evening of April 6, 1868, exactly nine months and six days after our country officially became the Dominion of Canada, the Hon. D'Arcy McGee, one of the finest orators ever to address the House of Commons, was at his eloquent best. A little after 2 a.m., the House adjourned. McGee, accompanied by Robert MacFarlane, a fellow Member of Parliament representing Perth, Ontario, left Parliament Hill. MacFarlane and McGee parted company at the corner of Metcalfe and Sparks. McGee walked towards his boarding house on the south side of Sparks between Metcalfe and O'Connor.

He reached his destination, the Toronto House at 71 Sparks St., owned and operated by Mary Ann Trotter. Mrs. Trotter, as was her custom, lay asleep on the cot in the dining room. She thought she heard a noise at the door. Believing it to be her son, thirteen-year-old Willie, a parliamentary page boy, she rose to open the door. Just as she did so, she witnessed the flash of a discharging revolver and saw the form of a man fall at her doorstep.

The Hon. Thomas D'Arcy McGee, one of the thirty-three Fathers of Confederation, was Canada's first murder victim. As he had bent over to insert his key into the lock of the boarding house door, his assailant silently pointed a revolver at the back of his neck. The Smith and Wesson revolver roared as the bullet entered McGee's neck and exited through his mouth. He died instantly.

In the days immediately following the assassination, several men were arrested as co-conspirators in the young country's most infamous single violent act. All would eventually be exonerated and released. All except one – James Whelan.

The bewhiskered Whelan had been employed in Ottawa as a tailor since November. He had previously followed his trade in Quebec City and Montreal.

When questioned within twenty-four hours of the assassination, he had a fully loaded revolver in his coat pocket. One chamber appeared to have been recently fired. Whelan was taken into custody. After a lengthy preliminary hearing, he was held over for trial.

On Sept. 7, 1868, Whelan stood trial for the murder of the Hon. D'Arcy McGee. News of the trial dwarfed all other events in the young Dominion. One of the founders of the country lay dead. His suspected killer came under microscopic examination.

The prosecution attorney, James O'Reilly, contended that Whelan had attended the House of Commons on the night of the murder, leaving before McGee. He had lain in wait for his victim in a gateway and had shot McGee in front of the door of his rooming house. O'Reilly claimed that the plot to kill McGee had been hatched in Montreal.

He asserted that Whelan had once visited McGee's home in Montreal. On that occasion he was met by John McGee, the victim's brother, and told him of a plot to set fire to the McGee residence. The threat was taken seriously and reported to police, although no attempt was ever made to set McGee's home on fire.

Most damaging of all, O'Reilly stated that someone, Jean Baptiste Lacroix, had actually witnessed the shooting. To back up his contentions, O'Reilly presented strong witnesses. John McGee confirmed Whelan's early morning visit to the McGee residence in Montreal.

Detective Edward O'Neill of Ottawa testified that he had found the .32 calibre revolver in the right-hand side pocket of Whelan's coat. In the opposite pocket he recovered a box of cartridges. Although the revolver was fully loaded when confiscated, O'Neill stated that upon examination it was clear to him that it had been recently fired.

"I looked in the cylinder and the six chambers, and I found six cartridges. Five of these cartridges looked like they'd been in there for some days. But one seemed to be put in recently." O'Neill went on to explain that one cartridge was bright, while the other five were dark and dull.

Jean Baptiste Lacroix told of walking home at the time of the murder. He saw a man at the door of the Toronto House and saw another man sneak up behind him. A shot rang out. The moon was full. Lacroix, from a distance of fifteen yards, saw the whole thing. When he heard the shot he stepped into the shadows. The assassin walked quickly past his place of concealment and Lacroix was able to identify him. It was James Whelan. Other witnesses took the stand, claiming that at various times they had overheard Whelan threaten to kill McGee.

Whelan was defended by the Hon. John Hillyard Cameron, believed by many to be the ablest lawyer in the country. The courtroom was silent. Shy, black-haired Euphemie Lafrance, a servant at Storr's Hotel on Clarence St., took the stand. When in Ottawa Whelan lived at the hotel.

Miss Lafrance stated that she knew Whelan, and that one of her duties was making up his bed. One morning she found a revolver under his mattress. She picked it up and it accidentally discharged, wounding her in the area of the left elbow. She displayed her scar to the court. Miss Lafrance claimed the accident occurred shortly before the McGee murder. This evidence effectively explained the reason for the one shiny bullet in Whelan's revolver.

Prosecution witness Lacroix's reputation was vigorously attacked. An array of tough lumberjacks who had known Lacroix for years took the stand and swore that the Crown's chief witness was a notorious liar. Their testimony had a forceful effect on the court, particularly when it was learned that Lacroix did not reveal his eye-witness account of the crime until he knew that a $20,000 reward had been offered for the apprehension and conviction of the killer.

The trial, attended by Prime Minister John A. MacDonald and his wife, lasted seven days. Whelan was found guilty. When asked if he had anything to say before sentence was passed, Whelan gave a long dissertation covering his history and the events of the night of the murder, all the while professing his innocence. He even absolved the jury for their wrong verdict, stating that based on the erroneous circumstantial evidence placed before them he too would have reached a guilty verdict.

On Thurs., Feb. 11, 1869, accompanied by Father John O'Connor, James Whelan walked directly to the scaffold built for his public execution. His last words were, "God save Ireland and God save my soul." Father O'Connor pressed a crucifix to the condemned man's lips. The trap door sprung open, the crowd gasped, and James Whelan was no more. His was the last public execution to take place in Canada.

A plaque commemorating D'Arcy McGee's assassination can still be seen opposite 143 Sparks St. in Ottawa.

PART SEVEN
WHO DONE IT?

TWILIGHT YEARS

Has the perfect murder ever been committed? I am alluding to those rare and mysterious cases of murder where all clues lead to a dead end. We have to go back in time to another day and another world to find such a pure murder mystery. Come along to the tranquility and pastoral beauty of rural England. You'll be presented with all the circumstances and clues left at the scene of the crime. You can even pass judgement on the one suspect in the case, much as Scotland Yard did so many years ago.

Major General Charles Edward Luard had served in the British Army for thirty years with the Royal Engineers. His distinguished military career concluded when he retired to lead the life of a country squire. His devoted wife was thrilled when the old warrior purchased a large brick manor house, Ightham Knoll, in beautiful Kent county. Situated on Maidstone Rd. between the quaint villages of Seal and Ightham, their home held nothing but promise for their twilight years.

Mrs. Luard, the daughter of a prosperous property owner, was quite accustomed to such a lifestyle. After so many years of leading the comfortable but unsettling life of an army officer's wife, she enjoyed every minute of retirement.

By 1908 the general was firmly entrenched as a country gentleman. He took an interest in local affairs, and sat on the Kent County Council. But it was strolling through the woods hand in hand with Mrs. Luard that the old gentleman loved most.

On Aug. 2, everything abruptly changed. Luard later gave a clear, concise statement of the events that unfolded that day.

At 2:30 p.m. Mr. and Mrs. Luard left their manor house to take a walk through the woods. Both had definite plans for the balance of the day. Accompanied by their Irish terrier, they crossed Fish Pond Woods, which was located on the property of their closest neighbour, Horace Wilkenson. They then took a footpath they had used many times before.

The general planned to continue to the Wildernesse Golf Course at Godden Green, which was about three miles from Ightham Knoll. Mrs. Luard planned to accompany her husband part way. She had told him that she expected an acquaintance, Mrs. Stewart, back at the manor house for tea, and would leave him around 3 o'clock for the return stroll home.

As they walked hand in hand through Fish Pond Woods they came upon Mr. Wilkenson's summer house. The couple had often had tea there that summer. They had just passed the empty summer house when Mrs. Luard felt it was time to return home to meet Mrs. Stewart. It was about 3 o'clock.

Luard reached the golf course at 3:25. He spoke to a member of the golf course staff at that time. Five minutes later the club house steward, Harry Kent, gave the general his golf clubs. The general practised a short while and then decided to walk home, using the road rather than the footpath through the woods. Rev. A.B. Cotton picked up Luard and the Irish terrier in his car and gave them a lift back to Ightham Knoll. They arrived home at precisely 4:30 p.m.

General Luard was shocked when he found his wife's guest, Mrs. Stewart, waiting at the house. Mrs. Luard had not returned home. She had left him at 3 o'clock and shouldn't have taken more than a half hour to return. The general had tea with Mrs. Stewart, feeling that his wife must have inexplicably been detained.

Finally, he could wait no longer. He went down to the footpath and started out once again on the route he had taken earlier that day. As he approached the Wilkenson's summer home he saw his wife's form stretched out on the veranda of the summer house. Thinking she had suffered a fall or had fainted, he rushed to her side. Mrs. Luard had not met with an accident. She had been brutally murdered.

Mrs. Luard's head lay in a pool of blood. Her left glove had been removed. The killer had obviously wrenched three valuable rings from her fingers. The glove was found inside out not far from the body. The glove on her right hand was in place and undisturbed. Strangely, someone had cut her entire pocket from her dress in order to remove her purse. General Luard ran to the Wilkensons'. He arrived there at 5:25 p.m. and gave the alarm.

Doctors examined the body at the scene. They noted that Mrs. Luard had been beaten about the head with some kind of stick or club. There were bruises and abrasions on the fingers of her left hand where someone had violently ripped away her rings. She had been shot twice with a small calibre revolver, once behind the right ear and once over the left temple. Powder burns were evident, indicating that she had been shot at close range. From the position of the body it was ascertained that the second bullet probably entered her head as she spun around in the act of falling. No club or revolver was found.

General Luard was genuinely distraught by the brutal murder of his wife. He was interrogated by the police and wrote out a statement that included all the facts as I have outlined them here. Every fact was verified by witnesses involved.

The crime was an unusually vicious one for peaceful Kent County. Scotland Yard uncovered two separate witnesses, who proved they had nothing whatever to do with the crime, but who were in the woods at the time of the murder. Both independently heard two shots at precisely 3:15 p.m. Detectives felt certain these were the shots that had killed Mrs. Luard.

160

Another witness, Thomas Durrant, a respected citizen of the area, had seen General Luard at 3:20 p.m., walking in the direction of the golf course. He was well over five minutes walking or running distance from the Wilkensons' summer home.

Who had killed Mrs. Luard and why?

Detectives walked and even ran the distances involved between manor house and summer home, and from summer home to golf course. The general and all the witnesses were telling the truth. It was impossible for him to have been at the summer home at 3:15, the time of the murder. He was just about at the golf course, having arrived there at 3:25. The general, the last known person to see his wife alive, was eliminated as a suspect.

Mrs. Luard had only been a couple of minutes beyond the summer house when she left her husband at 3 o'clock, yet she wasn't killed until 3:15. Police felt that, unknown to her husband, she may have been waiting for someone on the veranda of the summer house.

Police conducted an extensive search into the backgrounds of both the general and his wife. They were what they appeared to be – a retired, devoted couple with no known enemies.

Why did the murderer cut away a pocket containing the victim's purse? The purse could easily have been extracted from the pocket without cutting it. Scotland Yard had a theory. They felt it may have been an attempt to promote the murder for robbery motive. On the surface the cut-away pocket and the missing rings indicated robbery, but police thought that the killing was a cool calculated one made to look as if it had been committed during the commission of a robbery.

There were those who felt that a tramp may have just happened upon Mrs. Luard. Do tramps carry revolvers? Would a tramp cut away the pocket of a dead woman? Everyone seems to have seen General Luard that day. Surely someone would have spotted a stranger. All the surrounding villages were canvassed without uncovering anyone unusual.

161

Weeks went by and no progress was made in solving the case. The murder weapons were never found. Mrs. Luard's jewellery was never located.

Despite the evidence to the contrary, many believed that General Luard had murdered his wife. A steady stream of hate letters poured in to Ightham Knoll. The general read each one. He became so depressed that close friends feared for his health. One such friend, Col. Warde, invited the general to get away from it all and visit with him at his home near Maidstone. The general accepted the invitation, but the change didn't help.

On Sept. 17, the old gentleman could stand the harassment no longer. He threw himself into the path of an oncoming train. Luard left a suicide note to his friend Warde. In it he told of his unhappiness since the death of his wife, and how he now chose to join her rather than live without her. It was hardly the letter of a murderer.

Who killed Mrs. Luard? Why did they do it? The brutal murder that took place in Kent County in 1908 is as much a mystery today as it was the day after it was committed.

DID GRACE DO IT?

Unfortunately, factual murder mysteries do not always have the satisfactory conclusions associated with fiction. Case in point: the Croydon murders. I'll lay out the salient details of the murders and you can attempt to pick the murderer. Good luck, but I should warn you no one has conclusively solved this one in over fifty years of trying.

Our whodunnit took place during an eleven-month period beginning in April 1928 and concluding in March 1929. The locale was a respectable district of London known as Croydon, and involves two interrelated families, the Duffs and the Sidneys.

Edmund Duff had been employed as a civil servant in Nigeria for eighteen years before returning to England and settling down in a large comfortable home at 16 South Park Hill Rd., Croydon. His pension was not large, but allowed him and his wife Grace to enjoy a quiet, if frugal, lifestyle.

In 1928 Edmund was fifty-nine. The Duffs had three children, John, fourteen, Mary, twelve, and an infant. Maid Amy Clark completed the household.

On Monday, April 23, Edmund left to spend a short fishing vacation with an old crony in Fordingbridge, Hampshire. On Tuesday he phoned Grace and told her he would be returning home on Thursday. Edmund was met by Grace at

163

the South Croydon Station at 6:40 p.m. They arrived home within minutes.

Edmund complained of feeling feverish. The family physician, Dr. Robert Elwell, was phoned at 7:00 p.m. Meanwhile, the maid brought Edmund a hot meal and a bottle of beer. Edmund picked at the meal, but consumed the beer.

At 8:00 p.m. Dr. Elwell arrived, gave Edmund a cursory examination, but could find nothing wrong. Edmund mentioned that he had a slight headache and an extremely dry throat. Dr. Elwell prescribed aspirin and quinine. He left the Duff residence at 8:20 p.m.

About two hours later, Edmund and Grace went to bed. The Duffs slept in separate bedrooms. Throughout the night Grace thought she heard her husband vomit on several occasions.

Next morning Grace gave Edmund a cup of tea. He threw up immediately. Dr. Elwell was called, but was not available. His partner, Dr. John Binning, arrived at the Duff home around 12 p.m. Dr. Binning did not feel that Edmund's illness was serious. He stayed only five minutes.

After the doctor left, Edmund's condition worsened. He perspired and complained of stomach cramps. Dr. Binning looked in on his patient that afternoon and found that Edmund's condition had deteriorated. His hands and feet were ice cold. Binning left, but called Dr. Elwell to let him know that Edmund was very ill and could possibly be dying.

Binning then received a call from Grace. She was extremely agitated, stating that Edmund could hardly breathe. Binning headed for the Duff residence. When he arrived, Dr. Elwell was already there. Despite the actions of the two doctors, at 11 p.m. Edmund Duff breathed his last.

Both doctors agreed that they had no idea of the actual cause of death. An autopsy was performed, which indicated that no toxic substances were present in the body. Death was attributed to natural causes. Edmund was buried.

Grace Duff's single sister, Vera, and her widowed mother, Violet Sidney, lived only moments away at 29 Birdhurst Rise.

They employed a maid-cook, Mrs. Kathleen Noakes. Because they lived so close to Grace, it was natural that they visited often, especially after Grace lost her husband.

About nine months after Edmund's death, Vera felt ill. Her diary notations dated Jan. 1929, indicate that she was tired and generally unwell most of the month. Everyone liked Vera. She, in turn, at forty, devoted most of her time to her family. Grace and Vera had one brother, Tom Sidney, who was married and also lived close by.

On Mon., Feb. 11, Vera had supper with her mother. The meal consisted of warmed over vegetable soup, fish, potatoes, and pudding. Mrs. Sidney never took soup, but Vera had some, as did the cook, Mrs. Noakes. Both became ill and vomited throughout the night.

By Wednesday Vera and Mrs. Noakes appeared to have recovered. On Thursday Vera was again ill after taking a small quantity of soup. Dr. Elwell was called in by Grace Duff to attend to her sister. Grace was understandably worried and was continually popping in and out of 29 Birdhurst Rise.

Vera's condition deteriorated. On Fri., Feb. 15, she died. Dr. Elwell attributed the death to natural causes.

Mrs. Sidney now faced life in the large old home without the company of her daughter. It was small consolation to her that her daughter Grace and son Tom visited her every day.

On March 5, not quite three weeks after Vera's death, Mrs. Sidney took ill. She vomited violently, attributing her illness to Metatone, a medicine prescribed for her by Dr. Elwell. Mrs. Sidney had finished the bottle of Metatone that day and had commented on its bitter taste. Grace called Dr. Binning.

Tom Sidney dropped in and was startled to find his mother so ill. When he heard of his mother's suspicions concerning the Metatone, he suggested that Dr. Binning take charge of the empty bottle along with the wine glass from which the medication had been taken. That night at 7:25 Violet Sidney died.

An inquest was held into the untimely death. Rumours

now ran rampant throughout the community. Poor Grace Duff. She had lost her husband, sister, and mother, all within eleven months.

An autopsy on the body of Mrs. Sidney revealed traces of arsenic. Arsenic was also found in the Metatone bottle and the wine glass. Scotland Yard was called into the case. Vera's body was exhumed. Arsenic was found in her vital organs. Edmund Duff's body underwent a second post mortem. This time all organs tested were found to contain arsenic.

Clearly, someone had murdered three people in less than a year. But who? Bottles, jars, and tins were confiscated from the two homes. Weed killer containing arsenic was found in several containers, but this was not considered an unusual circumstance for homes with lawns.

Most important was the Metatone bottle. Obviously, someone had slipped poison into Mrs. Sidney's medicine. We may also conclude that one individual was responsible for all three murders.

Let's eliminate Amy Clark, the Duffs' maid. She was never in the Sidney home. The same goes for the Sidneys' maid, Mrs. Noakes, who was never in the Duff home. The Duffs' two children, John and Mary, were not present during their grandmother's illness. That leaves Dr. Elwell, Dr. Binning, Grace Duff, and Tom Sidney with the means and the opportunity to administer poison to all three victims.

Dr. Elwell was a fine, upstanding doctor with no possible motive for harming any of the three victims. The same cannot be said for Dr. Binning who, although married, was something of a ladies' man. It was felt that he had designs on Grace Duff, and some slight suspicion has been cast his way.

Tom Sidney came under serious suspicion. He was not a great fan of Edmund Duff's and stood to gain financially from the deaths of his sister and his mother, as did Grace Duff.

Pick whoever you fancy, but for my money Grace Duff was the culprit. Her husband Edmund, from all reports, was not an easy man to live with. She may have tired of her life with him and seized the opportunity to murder him when he arrived home from his fishing trip complaining of illness. She could easily have put the arsenic in his beer at any time.

Once she got the hang of it, she may have murdered her sister and mother to speed up her inheritance. She probably put the arsenic in her sister's soup and her mother's medicine. Grace was at each of the three deathbeds, a practice that gives perverted pleasure to some poisoners. At the death of her husband Grace inherited £1,200. When Vera died she inherited £2,000. On her mother's death she inherited £5,500, large sums in 1929.

No one was ever brought to trial for the Croydon Poison Mystery. Maybe the answer to it was lost forever on June 24, 1973, the day Grace Duff died. She was 87.

THE PERFECT
MURDER

To get away with murder is no easy task, but it does happen. The most successful murder of all, at least from the perpetrator's point of view, is a death that is never detected as murder. The untimely demise is attributed to an accident or natural causes and is never investigated. There is another category, where the act of murder is obvious, but every investigative avenue leads to a dead end and the murderer goes free.

Nora Fuller was an unlikely victim. In 1902 she was a teenager, looking for a job, preferably in the entertainment industry. She had performed on the stage in high school, and applied for any job openings involving the theatre. Work wasn't easy to come by. After some weeks she decided to take a stop-gap job. That's how she came to answer an advertisement in a San Francisco newspaper: "Young girl to take care of baby; good home and good wages; Box 120 – Chronicle."

The next day Nora received a postcard: "Miss Fuller, In answer to yours in response to my advt., kindly call at the Popular Restaurant, 55 Geary St., and inquire for Mr. John Bennett at 1 o'clock. If you can't come at 1, come at 6. J.B."

Nora had to rush to get to the restaurant by six. She grabbed an apple, said goodbye to her mother and brother, and hurried out of the house to keep her appointment. An hour later, her brother Louis answered the phone. It was

Nora. She told her brother that she had met Mr. Bennett, and was starting work immediately at his residence at 1500 Geary St. Louis shouted the news to his mother and said goodbye.

At about 5:30 that same day, Mr. Krone, the owner of the Popular Restaurant, was told by one of his patrons that he was expecting a young girl to call on him. The man asked Krone to send her to his table. After waiting a half hour he left the restaurant and was seen pacing up and down outside the front door. Krone later stated that the man in question had often eaten in his establishment. He was about forty years old, five feet eight, and weighed about 160 pounds. He had a brown moustache, and was always well-dressed.

When Nora failed to return that night, her mother reported her missing to the police. After a complete investigation they assumed that Nora had kept her appointment with Mr. John Bennett, but from there it appeared as if Nora had fallen off the edge of the earth. John Bennett didn't exist. The address at 1500 Geary St. was a vacant lot. With no new clues coming in, the investigation wound down.

On Feb. 8, almost a month after Nora ran out of her house eating an apple, her body was found. A real estate representative, whose job it was to inspect houses before renting them to new tenants, was to scrutinize a house at 2211 Sutter St. The house had been rented for one month, which would be up the following day. The real estate agent went through the property, which appeared never to have been occupied by the previous tenant. He gingerly opened the door to a tiny back room. Inside, lying on a bed, was the nude, mutilated body of a young girl. The real estate agent ran from the vacant house directly to the first policeman he could find. The dead girl was Nora Fuller.

Investigating detectives learned of the efforts that had been made to trace the missing girl, and how that investigation had bogged down. They learned that two days before the advertisement appeared in the *Chronicle*, a Mr. C.D. Hawkins had leased the house on Sutter St. from the real estate firm of Umsen and Co. When questioned about references, Hawkins stated that he and his wife had been living in a hotel for years. To circumvent any inconvenience, he would pay the first month's rent in advance. Money talks. The deal was consummated then and there. The salesman from Umsen & Co. described his client as being about forty years old, five foot eight inches, well dressed, and having a brown moustache. Obviously Hawkins and Bennett were the same man.

Hawkins' movements were traced further. He purchased furniture on the same day that he rented the house. He systematically went about outfitting one room, the room in which Nora Fuller was to die. He paid cash and demanded that his furniture be delivered that same night. Pillows, sheets, and blankets were purchased from another store. All were paid for by cash with the stipulation that they be delivered immediately. Both stores did deliver their wares to the empty, eerie house. The delivery men were met by Hawkins and led to the little back room. The bed was set up. The following night Nora Fuller was to occupy it.

The vacant house and the murder room were examined without concrete results. Attempts to trace the murderer proved frustrating. All efforts came to an abrupt stop with the purchase of the furniture and the bedclothing. Even the original postcard was missing. Nora had taken it with her on her appointment with death. The killer had taken it from her purse. The details of the card were provided by Nora's mother.

An autopsy revealed that Nora had been strangled. Her last intake of food was the apple she had taken from her house. She had been killed on the same day. The vacant house had no water or gas hookup. No fire had been lit in the fireplace. It became obvious that the killer had placed the ad, leased the house, and bought the furniture all for one night's use.

After a frustrating investigation, the police got a break. A clerk, Charles B. Hadley, had disappeared. His employer reported that Hadley had been fixing the books and that he was several thousand dollars short. Hadley's girlfriend, Ollie

Blasier, told the police that her boyfriend had flown the coop immediately after Nora Fuller's disappearance. One day he just walked out on her. Another interesting bit of information was that Charlie habitually wore a false moustache. He fit the description of Bennett-Hawkins. When the killer, using the name Hawkins, leased the house on Sutter St., he had to sign a document. Ollie Blazier came up with Hadley's signature on a photograph he had given her. The two signatures were compared and were both written by the same man.

Hadley had worked for fourteen years at the same job. In recent years he had lived with Miss Blasier. Even she was amazed to find out how little she knew about him. Hadley was a loner. The police were unable to trace anyone who could shed any light on his past.

The man who had set the stage for murder, and killed his victim, effectively disappeared and has never been found or punished. He had committed the perfect murder.

LYDIA LOST HER
HEAD

The city of Detroit, Michigan, has long been associated with murder. The incidence of homicide per capita in Detroit is one of the highest of any city in the world. It takes more than a run of the mill murder to jar the citizens of the automobile city, accustomed as they are to murder on a daily basis. The Lydia Thompson case caught and held their attention for months.

Lydia was born in Russia. At the end of World War I she met Victor Thompson in Constantinople, where he was stationed with the British Army and where she was employed as a nurse. The attractive pair married and headed for Detroit to start a new life. From the very beginning they prospered. Vic gravitated toward the automobile industry, and eventually came to own a profitable agency. In addition, the couple owned a laundry and a garage.

In keeping with their financial success, they acquired an impressive executive home in Orchard Lake, an exclusive area just outside the city. The Thompson home had all the amenities of affluence – a swimming pool, tennis courts, pool tables, and well-stocked bars. To an outsider or even a casual acquaintance, it appeared that the Thompson's long marriage had been made in heaven. From Lydia's point of view the union may have been created in more nether regions.

By 1945 Lydia, at forty-seven, had begun to notice those

telltale gray hairs and wrinkles on her otherwise attractive visage. It seemed to her that Vic stayed away from home more often with each passing month. Things had not gone well since the beginning of the Second World War. Cars were in short supply, and Vic's business activities slowed down. As a result, he had time on his hands, and it appeared to Lydia that her husband chose to spend this time away from her.

Lydia accused her husband of engaging in dalliances with other women. The situation was so bad that Vic's comings and goings became an obsession with his wife. Lydia would stay in her home for weeks on end crying and otherwise making herself miserable. Her only conversation with friends was about her husband. She would pour out her troubles to anyone who would listen.

Instead of bringing Vic closer, her possessive nature drove him further afield. One of the directions Vic headed toward was Helen Budnik. Helen had at one time been Thompson's secretary, but the working friendship had soon developed into a far closer and warmer relationship.

The more Lydia nagged, the more Vic ran to Helen's welcoming arms. Lydia became so distraught she had detectives follow her husband. She didn't believe their reports, and ended up tailing the detectives herself. A few classic confrontations took place between Lydia and Helen. Helen told Lydia she couldn't help it if Vic didn't love her anymore. To these expressions of comfort, Helen added that maybe Lydia should stop bugging Vic. Despite this warning, Lydia kept on making herself and everyone around her miserable.

On Oct. 13, 1945, the turbulent domestic lives of Lydia, Vic, and Helen made front-page news. That was the day three mushroom pickers found the body of Lydia Thompson in a lonely marsh, not far from suburban Pontiac. Someone had cut off her head. She had icepick stab marks on her chest and back.

Investigating officers questioned Vic Thompson and Helen Budnik, both of whom came under suspicion from the moment the body was found. They readily told the police of their relationship with the dead woman, and claimed they had nothing to do with Lydia's death. Both took lie detector tests, which indicated they were telling the truth; and both had airtight alibis for the night of Lydia's murder. Vic and Helen were released from custody after questioning.

Lydia's diary was found. It revealed the hopeless situation that existed between her and her husband. The diary was of no help in identifying her murderer, but it did indicate that she had a premonition of her death. She made several references to this in her diary and had even purchased a gun for protection.

An extensive search of the area where the body was discovered was conducted by Boy Scouts in an effort to find the murder weapon, but it was never found. A purse that Lydia usually carried was also missing.

The murder investigation wound down, as no new clues to the mystery were uncovered. Four months after the murder, in February 1946, Vic married Helen Budnik. While Vic was cleaning his home in preparation for his new wife's occupancy, he moved an icebox. Out popped his dead wife's purse. Later he found Lydia's gun in a little-used cupboard. Both of these discoveries shed no light on the identity of the killer.

There were no new developments for another year, but many thought that Vic, acting alone, or with Helen's help, had murdered his first wife. Seventeen months after the murder, Mr. and Mrs. Thompson were arrested and charged with Lydia's murder. The police had come up with a pots and pans peddler who claimed he had been hired by Vic to do the actual killing. The obvious motive was to get rid of Lydia in order to marry Helen.

There was one little catch. It was proven in court that the pots and pans peddler was lying. He had concocted the whole story to scare his girlfriend. Charges against the accused pair were dropped. The Thompsons were released.

And that's where the case stands to this day.

WAS CAPTAIN HART GUILTY?

It is doubtful that many people have heard of Tenants Harbour, Maine. Situated about ten miles from Thomaston, Tenants Harbour is a quaint little crossroads by the sea. Nothing of interest has ever happened there, with one exception.

In 1877 the village was the scene of one of New England's most famous and mysterious murders. Five years later, in nearby Massachusetts, a young lady named Lizzie Borden was to stand accused of taking an axe and chopping up her mother and father. The Borden case was to become one of the most written about and analyzed crimes ever perpetrated, while the Sarah Meservey case of Tenants Harbour has been relegated to dim memory.

Before the turn of the century inhabitants along the coast of Maine were primarily sailors. They would take off from the northeast coast of the U.S. in schooners and travel the world. Voyages lasting over a year were not uncommon.

In October 1877 Captain Luther Meservey boarded his schooner, the Bickmore, for a four-month long sea voyage. His thirty-seven-year-old wife Sarah was quite accustomed to her husband's lengthy absences. Sarah, a slim, tall, no-nonsense woman quickly fell into her usual routine when the captain was at sea. She knitted, sewed, and cleaned the house.

175

Chores neglected for months were now completed. Seldom did she leave her home other than to make her regular pilgrimage to the post office each day to collect her mail.

Two months passed without any changes. But Dec. 22 was to be the last day of Sarah Meservey's life. It was a Saturday. As dusk was falling over Tenants Harbour, Sarah walked down the street to the post office. Once there she learned that her neighbour, Mark Wall, had picked up her mail. Sometimes he brought her mail home with him and she would pick it up later at his house.

Sarah started off on the five-minute walk home. She paused and passed the time of day with a few friends on the way. She decided not to pick up her mail that evening. Instead she entered her house and closed the door.

Next morning Mark Wall sent his young son to Sarah's house with her mail. The boy noticed that the curtains were drawn, which was rather unusual. He pounded on the door, but received no reply.

In the days that followed, Sarah Meservey didn't take part in the Christmas activities of the village. Snow fell. No one cleared a path to Sarah's door. Mail piled up for her down at the post office.

It wasn't until Jan. 29, a good five weeks since Sarah was last seen, that anything was done. The lack of curiosity exhibited by the inhabitants of Tenants Harbour is one of the mysteries surrounding the Meservey case. It is almost beyond comprehension that in such a small community not one person would act after a few days, let alone five weeks. No mention or reason for this time lapse is reported in the many newspaper accounts of the case, which was covered extensively at the time of the crime. We can only assume that small towns and villages are more private places than we are led to believe.

On Jan. 29, Captain Albion Meservey, a cousin of Sarah's husband, brought the matter of her absence to the attention of a village politician, one Whitney Long. The two men crawled through a window into the freezing Meservey residence. Entering the bedroom the men found the floor strewn with glass from a broken mirror. Furniture was overturned and a great deal of blood was on the floor and walls. In the middle of the room was the frozen body of Sarah Meservey, rolled snugly into a quilt.

Next day the coroner reported that a scarf had been wrapped around Sarah's neck, causing death by strangulation. Several bruises were evident about the head. The victim's hands were tied behind her back with cod line. The knots themselves were obviously seamen's knots. Sarah had been fully clothed in an overcoat and overshoes when she met her death. This indicated that she had been killed shortly after she had returned from the post office weeks before. Bloody handprints were all over the house. On the kitchen floor police found a note that was almost illegible. Dated Dec. 24, the letter stated that the killer hadn't murdered Sarah for money, but for some other reason that he didn't state. Despite the note, the house had been ransacked. Police believed Sarah had surprised her killer in the act of robbing the house. The residents of Tenants Harbour were aghast at the thought that one of them was a killer.

On Feb. 16, Captain Luther Meservey returned home to learn of his wife's murder.

Three days later Mrs. Levi Hart received a letter from Philadelphia dated Feb. 10 and postmarked Feb. 16. The letter urged her husband, who was actively helping the police in their investigation, to stop assisting the authorities. It also stated that the killer would never be apprehended. Police believed that the letter had been written by a citizen of Tenants Harbour who had managed to have it mailed from Philadelphia.

Sherriff A.T. Lowe, in charge of the investigation from the outset, had four local men write out a phrase that had been included in the first letter found on Sarah's kitchen floor. The phrase was "i kiled her." Based on a handwriting comparison the Sherriff arrested Captain Nathan F. Hart.

As time went on it became common knowledge that Sherriff Lowe had found a particular type of wooden match on the floor of the Meservey kitchen. In the entire village, only Capt. Nathan Hart used this distinctive type of match.

Capt. Hart stood trial for murder on Oct. 1, 1878. He swore he knew nothing of the murder of Sarah Meservey. Prosecuting attorneys attempted to prove that Capt. Hart couldn't account for his actions on the evening of Dec. 22 when he had strangled Sarah with her scarf. Worried about this, the Captain sneaked back into the house on Dec. 24 and planted the note dated the 24th so that police would be led to believe the murder took place on that date. The Captain had an ironclad alibi for the evening of Dec. 24.

The prosecution pressed on. They were able to produce witnesses who swore that Capt. Hart had discussed the murder before the body was found. He had also described conditions that existed inside the house to other residents of the village.

Why would Capt. Hart want to kill his friend and neighbour? The prosecution came up with a witness who claimed the Captain had made improper advances to Sarah some six months before the murder and had been repulsed.

The prosecution hit a snag when they attempted to prove that Capt. Hart had written both the letter found on the kitchen floor and the one sent from Philadelphia. The handwriting expert, a Professor Dutton, who had caused Capt. Hart to be arrested in the first place, now appeared in court for the defence. It appears that a ship's log, purportedly written by Capt. Hart, had been used as a sample of his handwriting to be compared to the two incriminating letters. Prof. Dutton still claimed all three documents were written by the same man. The fly in the ointment was that the ship's log had been written not by Capt. Nathan Hart, but by Capt. Albion Meservey. Prof. Dutton had gone to the trouble of bringing in other experts to corroborate his startling findings.

Capt. Hart answered his accusers from the witness stand. He stated that he had dreamed that Sarah had been murdered. He also dreamed of the conditions inside the Meservey house, a not altogether impossible feat considering the conjecture running rampant through the village just before the body was found. Capt. Hart admitted he didn't have an alibi for Dec. 22. He simply was at home that night and hadn't been seen by anyone. He did state, and had his evidence corroborated by a friend, that on Dec. 24 he had been afoot with his friend taking a gift to his granddaughter, who lived in a neighbouring village. Not too far from Sarah Meservey's house they had seen a stranger approaching from the opposite direction. The night had been snowy and the misty figure unrecognizable. The stranger seemed to be holding a coat over his head. Capt. Hart thought nothing more of the stranger until the body was discovered and he was arrested.

After only two hours deliberation the jury returned a verdict of guilty of murder in the first degree. As there was no death penalty in Maine at the time, Capt. Hart was sentenced to life imprisonment at Thomaston, Maine.

There were many who believed that Hart was innocent. Strong suspicion pointed to Capt. Albion Meservey as the writer of the two letters and the actual murderer. Prof. Dutton worked tirelessly on behalf of the convicted man. He wrote books, gave lectures, and generally kept the case alive as the years passed. Capt. Albion Meservey further complicated matters by stating that he too thought Capt. Hart innocent. Of course he swore he was not the author of the letters, and certainly not the killer.

On Oct. 9, 1883, after five years imprisonment, Capt. Nathan Hart died. His body was transported back to Tenants Harbour for burial. The entire village turned out for the funeral. Among the mourners was Hart's staunchest supporter, Prof. Dutton, who swore to his dying day that an innocent man had been imprisoned for a crime he did not commit.

179

In the five years after Sarah's murder, the Meservey case and its rather unsatisfactory conclusion was the chief topic of conversation in New England. Then that God-fearing, church-going young lady named Borden "took an axe and gave her mother forty whacks." Everybody stopped talking about Sarah and began talking about Lizzie. You see, Lizzie was alive, and Sarah was very very dead.

PART EIGHT
THE POISONERS

THE CONNECTICUT HOUSEWIFE

I drove through the lush Connecticut countryside towards the small town of Derby. It is difficult to imagine that this peaceful community tucked away on the side of a hill along the Housatonic River was once the home of one of the most prolific female mass murderers in the history of the U.S. It was here that Lydia Sherman ended her career of dispensing arsenic with a degree of abandonment rarely experienced before or since.

Lydia's infamous history can be traced back to 1847, when she married a policeman, Edward Struck, in New York City. The marriage was to last for seventeen years, during which Lydia gave birth to six handsome children: Lydia, Anne Eliza, William, George, Edward, and Mary Ann.

After such a lengthy period of marital bliss, an incident occurred on the streets of New York that was to have far reaching effects on the Struck family. Edward was abruptly dismissed from the Metropolitan Police Force. Evidently there was some question concerning Struck's reaction under pressure. It was reported that he hurriedly left the scene of a disturbance, leaving a citizen to disarm a madman in a saloon.

Lydia was not only furious; she was embarrassed and ashamed. She began making excuses for her husband. He was ill, he was insane – anything that came to mind.

Meanwhile, Lydia had to face the practical problem of feeding her children. Lydia obtained a position as a nurse to Dr. L.A. Rodenstein. It was while employed with Dr. Rodenstein that Lydia first became acquainted with arsenic and its lethal qualities.

One glorious day in May 1864, Lydia dropped into a Harlem drug store and purchased a quantity of arsenic. She explained to the druggist that her apartment was "alive with rats." What better way to rid herself of the wee beasties than a good dose of arsenic. The deadly powder cost her ten cents.

That night Lydia cooked up a batch of warm oatmeal for Edward. It didn't agree with him at all. Within hours he was confined to bed. Lydia was concerned. She nursed him all night, attempting to relieve his agony with assorted medicines. She even endeavoured to bolster his strength with more oatmeal, but Edward had lost his appetite.

In the morning Edward was in such bad shape that Lydia called in a neighbouring physician, Dr. N. Hustead. At this point in Lydia's saga it is rather strange that no one wondered why she didn't summon her employer, Dr. Rodenstein, but at the time no one gave it a second thought.

At any rate, it was too late for Edward. He died in agony before Dr. Hustead arrived at his bedside. Lydia was overcome with grief at her loss. The good doctor could scarcely stand the way she carried on. She suggested that "consumption carried poor Edward away." Dr. Hustead agreed, and signed the death certificate accordingly.

Once Lydia got the hang of the poisoning business, there was no stopping her. In the following months she proceeded to annihilate all six of her own children. July 5 seems to have been a red-letter day: on that day she killed three of her offspring.

By the time the second anniversary of Edward's demise rolled around, the entire family was dead and buried. Lydia was clever enough to employ various doctors, all of whom attributed the rash of deaths to natural causes.

Only one man was suspicious. Rev. Mr. Payson of the

Harlem Presbyterian Church, who had watched Lydia, the eldest Struck daughter, die in agony, couldn't get certain evil thoughts out of his mind. Several days after young Lydia's death he passed his suspicions along to the District Attorney's office. The D.A. failed to act.

Through an acquaintance, Lydia secured a position in Stratford, Connecticut, as nurse and housekeeper to a Mrs. Curtiss. There seems little doubt that Mrs. Curtiss was ripe for one of Lydia's little white powders, but the old lady proved to be a crusty, intelligent New Englander who wouldn't be bamboozled. Lydia let it be known around Stratford that she was available for employment elsewhere if the opportunity presented itself.

Eight uneventful months passed. One day, while grocery shopping in John Fairchild's store, Lydia was told by Mr. Fairchild that an old gentleman named Dennis Hurlbut of Corum, Connecticut had just lost his wife and was looking for a housekeeper. When Lydia learned that Hurlbut was over seventy-five years old and was reputed to be wealthy, she required no further encouragement.

Lydia dashed over to Corum, now known as Shelton. Hurlbut, who was approaching senility, expected an old lady with whom to argue away his remaining years. The old dog was smitten the moment he laid eyes on attractive, trim, 44-year-old Lydia.

Within a week Hurlbut proposed. The odd couple were married on Nov. 22, 1868. Lydia played the industrious housekeeper and loving wife to the hilt. Three months after the knot was tied, Hurlbut made his will.

Eleven months later Lydia, complete in widow's weeds, buried her second husband. Old Hurlbut's demise left Lydia a wealthy woman by 1870 standards. She became the sole owner of her late husband's farm, as well as of cash amounting to $10,000.

Today, over 112 years since the murder, you can still find the record of the unsuspecting Hurlbut's death in the registry of births, deaths, and marriages, at the Shelton Town Hall.

Under cause of death is the ominous notation – arsenic poisoning.

Lydia always seemed to be in the right place at the right time when it came to members of the opposite sex. This time, Mr. William Thomas, who delivered the mail to Lydia's farm, told the brand new widow that a man named Nelson Sherman of Derby had just lost his wife and was left with four children. He was in dire need of a housekeeper. Lydia indicated that she was interested, even though her true love, old Hurlbut, was scarcely two months removed from this mortal coil.

A meeting was arranged. Nelson Sherman, who held down a good job with a Derby tack manufacturer, was delighted at the prospect of having good-looking Lydia as his housekeeper, and who knows, maybe even much more.

He explained to Lydia that he had an infant son and three other children at home. Besides his offspring, he was stuck with his deceased wife's mother, Mrs. Mary Jones. His mother-in-law simply didn't get along with his children, and things were going from bad to worse. His fourteen-year-old daughter Ada and Mrs. Jones were at each other's throats constantly. Horatio, eighteen, Nattie, four, and Frank, the nine-month-old baby, rounded out the household.

In the ensuing months Nelson wooed the widow Hurlbut. This time, with old Hurlbut's coin rattling in her pockets, Lydia was in no particular rush to wed. However, when she felt the time was right, she once more let herself be led to the altar.

On Sept. 2, 1870, Lydia became Mrs. Nelson Sherman. Things did not proceed smoothly from the very first day. The mother-in-law proved to be an ornery old woman, who relished arguing with young Ada. Baby Frank was a handful. Slowly it dawned on Lydia that by marrying Nelson Sherman she had bitten off more than she could chew.

One day, completely frustrated at the direction events were taking in his household, Nelson blurted out that he wished baby Frank were dead. Then his dear old mother-in-law would have no further reason for staying on.

The cool waters of the Housatonic River flowed gently past the Shermans' white house the day Lydia heard this very practical suggestion. Her ears perked up. A twinkle came to her eye. Did someone suggest a death in the family might be beneficial?

Lydia strained to hear. Yes, she was positive – there were rats scurrying about in the attic. She must fetch some arsenic and get rid of the nasty little devils.

Quick as a wink, Frank became ill. He simply couldn't hold anything in his stomach. Small wonder. Lydia had laced the baby's milk with arsenic. To put it in her own words, "I was full of trouble, and not knowing what to do, I put some arsenic in his milk."

Mother-in-law Mary Jones grew alarmed, and sent for Dr. A. Beardsley, the family physician, who lived a few doors away from the Shermans. Dr. Beardsley arrived at the house in the morning, took one look at Frank, and declared that the child was suffering from colic. The doctor gave the sick child several medicines. By late afternoon the baby appeared to be recovering slowly. Lydia put a stop to all that. When the doctor left, she gave little Frank some of her own medicine. Frank was dead by 11 o'clock that night.

Around this time it is quite possible that Nelson Sherman had some inkling that he had married a monster. Always a man who liked his whiskey, Nelson took to the bottle with a vengeance. Rarely did he show up at the tack factory where he was employed. In fact, at this juncture in his life, Nelson was pretty well in the sauce all the time. He had good reason.

During the holiday season of 1870 a heavy snowfall descended on the peaceful little village of Derby. Sleighs pulled by proud horses, gaily decorated with Christmas bells, dashed through the centre of the town. No one was aware that in their tranquil community dwelt a mass murderer who poisoned without feeling or remorse. Lydia had by now chalked up nine victims.

That Christmas, Nelson's daughter Ada was busy helping

the Rev. Morton decorate the tree down at the Congregational Church. Unaccountably, Ada became so ill that Rev. Morton sent her home. Lydia felt that Ada had partaken of too much candy, but Rev. Morton thought the matter much more serious.

He was so concerned that he showed up at the Sherman residence later that afternoon with Dr. Beardsley, the same doctor who had unsuccessfully treated Ada's brother Frank. Dr. Beardsley prescribed brandy for his patient. Ada lived through the night.

Lydia was later to state, "I felt so bad I was tempted to do as I had done before. I had some arsenic in the house and I mixed some in her tea and gave it to her twice. She died the next morning."

After the death of his second child, Nelson Sherman stayed drunk all the time. Things were not going well for Lydia, who was financing Nelson's drunken sprees in New Haven. But to every cloud there is a silver lining. Nelson's mother-in-law moved out.

Lydia's joy at seeing Mary Jones depart was diluted by Nelson's unquenchable thirst. Now a confirmed drunk, he no longer shared her bed. In short, he became an absolute bore.

One fine day in April, Lydia hitched up her wagon and, together with five-year-old Nattie, drove over to the village of Birmingham. She pulled in front of the Birmingham Drug Store and walked inside with Nattie. Mr. Peck, the proprietor, waited on Lydia, who stated, "We are overrun with rats. What is best to kill them?"

Mr. Peck suggested several patent poisons, but in the end added that, "Arsenic is cheaper and just as good." Lydia chose arsenic.

When Lydia returned home Nelson was away in New Haven, dissipating $300 he had received from selling the family piano. Lydia waited for her husband's return for several days before dispatching Horatio, the eldest son, to bring his father back to Derby. After much saloon searching, Horatio located his father and brought him back.

Nelson immediately had an attack of stomach cramps. Lydia was up to her old tricks. "I had about a pint of brandy in the house, and I put some arsenic in it. That night he drank some of the brandy, and the next morning he was very sick."

For the next few days Nelson continued to suffer. Dr. Beardsley was called in. He attributed Nelson's trouble to his excessive drinking. The patient grew weaker. Dr. Beardsley brought in a colleague, Dr. Pinny, but Nelson continued to deteriorate. Nelson lasted a week before expiring.

It was now all too much for Dr. Beardsley. He had been the attending physician at three Sherman deaths. Despite the grieving wife, despite the alcoholic husband, something was wrong. All three deaths had been accompanied by similar symptoms – dry mouth, nausea, vomiting, stomach pain, faintness, and great thirst, all symptoms compatible with arsenic poisoning.

Dr. Beardsley actually was bold enough to ask Lydia if she had given her husband arsenic. Lydia was aghast. Heavens no, she replied. The concerned doctor then asked for permission to perform an autopsy. Lydia consented.

On Saturday, the day after Nelson's death, his liver and stomach were rattling along the New Haven railroad, on the way to Yale University to be examined. The next day the bodies of Ada and Frank Sherman, as well as Dennis Hurlbut, were exhumed. Their vital organs were sent to Yale as well.

On Monday, before the results of the tests for arsenic were returned to Derby, Lydia took off for New Brunswick, New Jersey, where detectives took her into custody. She was returned to Derby, and later transferred to New Haven, to stand trial for the murder of Nelson Sherman. Meanwhile, doctors had examined the vital organs of Nelson, Ada, and Frank Sherman, as well as those of Dennis Hurlbut. All were laced with arsenic.

Lydia Sherman's trial for murder began on April 16, 1872. Throughout the several months of her incarceration at Derby, she steadfastly maintained her innocence. Her case captured the imagination of the entire country. It was a rare day that curious onlookers and reporters didn't hover about the Derby jail, hoping for a glimpse of the "Birmingham Borgia."

Lydia's trial lasted ten days, and concluded with her being found guilty of murder in the second degree and being sentenced to life imprisonment. While in jail awaiting her lawyer's attempts to obtain a new trial, Lydia dramatically confessed in detail to killing six of her own children, her three husbands, and the two Sherman children, in all, eleven murders.

Despite her admissions, she did not give detailed motives for her horrible crimes. Students of the Sherman case believe Lydia did away with Dennis Hurlbut, her second husband, to gain his wealth. In her confession, she mentioned that she killed several of the children so they would be "better off."

Lydia was imprisoned in the Connecticut State Prison for five and a half years, until her death on May 16, 1878.

THE MAD SCIENTIST

Ladies and gentlemen who have had the opportunity and ability to gain a higher education should know better than to go around killing people. Yet we have only to glance at the record to find that learned gentlemen such as Dr. Webster didn't bat an eyelash while disposing of Dr. Parkman within the hallowed precincts of Harvard University. Then there was lawyer Lincoln Alexander, who not only murdered his wife and brother-in-law, but had the gall to pulverize their bodies, mix the remains with fertilizer and sprinkle the result over his sweet peas.

Eric Muenter was born in Germany, where he lived until he was almost twenty. Something of a ladies' man, Eric had no difficulty finding companionship on any given evening. One young woman wanted more than a one-night stand; Eric married her and almost immediately realized the error of his ways. He promptly deserted the temporary love of his life and took off for Chicago, U.S.A.

Eric, a high school graduate in Germany, had no difficulty enrolling at the University of Chicago. In 1899 he received his Bachelor of Arts degree with honours and accepted a teaching job in the city.

His future secure, Eric looked around for a suitable companion with whom he could share the good life. Almost immediately he met Leone Krembs, who not only was beautiful, but was from a wealthy family. Leone and Eric were soon married.

Before long the union was blessed by the arrival of a baby girl. In 1904, Professor Muenter applied for and was accepted as a German instructor at Harvard.

Once established in the Ivy League, Eric became an early-day hippie. A skinny six-footer, he wobbled like a duck when he walked, wore a nondescript felt hat that came down over his ears, and had an unruly growth of beard. He also seemed to have an aversion to soap and water. No question about it, Eric was considered a character around campus.

On April 10, 1906, Leone gave birth to the couple's second child. She had no medical assistance, and while the baby did well, Leone died six days after the birth with only Eric at her side to comfort her. The grieving husband had some difficulty obtaining his doctor's signature on the death certificate.

In due course the death was brought to the attention of the Chief Medical Officer, Dr. Swan. He performed an autopsy.

The doctor was not a dummy. Before returning the body to Eric for burial the clever medic informed him that he had taken the precaution of extracting the stomach and dispatching it to the Harvard Medical School for examination. In the meantime Eric quickly had the rest of Leone cremated. Then, realizing what the toxicological analysis would disclose, he placed his two children with his in-laws in Chicago and took off. Sure enough, the examination of Leone's stomach revealed enough arsenic to kill a horse.

The hunt for the murderer was extensive. Eric's exploits received wide publicity, but the tall, weird-looking instructor had managed to disappear. He changed his name to Frank Holt and made his way to Mexico, where he altered his appearance by shaving his face and head. Under his new name he gained employment with the huge Krupp Munitions Works. No doubt our hero could have remained in Mexico in safety the rest of his life, but he saw himself only as a teacher and would settle for nothing less.

In Feb. 1908 Frank Holt entered the Fort Worth Polytechnical Institute as a freshman. He amazed the entire institution by completing four years of college in one year, attaining his Bachelor of Arts degree in June 1909, again graduating with honours. Frank Holt joined the staff of the Fort Worth Polytechnical Institute as a German instructor.

Miss Sensabaugh, a well-endowed student of the weird professor, was the recipient of individual instruction of a more intimate nature. Soon the lovers married and promptly became the parents of one, then another, little Holt. The Holts lived happily enough until 1912.

From Fort Worth the family moved to Ithaca, New York, where Frank enrolled in Cornell University. Here this amazing academic obtained his Ph.D. It was also at Cornell that his luck ran out. A visiting professor from Chicago recognized the former Eric Muenter. Later, the professor admitted that after giving the matter some thought he decided that after so many years nothing would be gained by turning in the obviously reformed man. The old professor was wrong. Dr. Holt had only begun his infamous career as a criminal.

In June 1915, Dr. Holt told his colleagues and family that he was taking a vacation. The professor purchased two revolvers in a pawn shop in New Jersey, and then proceeded to pick up two hundred sticks of dynamite, together with all the paraphernalia needed to manufacture a time bomb.

Working out of rented quarters in Long Island, the demented academic made several bombs. He sent some by express to England. Then Dr. Holt embarked on his amazing weekend. He packed his dynamite factory in a large trunk and hopped the train for New York. In addition he lugged a suitcase, which contained several deadly bombs. The trunk was stored in a warehouse while Dr. Holt continued on to Washington with his suitcase. He made his way to the outer office of the vice president of the United States, where he secreted one of his infernal packages. The bomb exploded while the doctor was many miles away returning to New York by train. No one was hurt by the blast, but the fact that

192

someone could plant a bomb in such a well-secured locale was cause for concern.

Meanwhile Holt managed to dash off a few letters to newspapers, in which he revealed the reason for the bomb. It was to attract attention to the fact that munitions manufacturers were supplying arms to the Allied Forces in Europe. Obviously the learned professor was not rowing with both oars in the water.

Back in Long Island, Holt made his way to the estate of J. Pierpont Morgan. Dr. Holt had difficulty getting to see the influential financier because of a suspicious butler. When Holt pulled a revolver the butler still managed to warn Morgan and several dinner guests that a madman was loose in the house. In the confusion that followed, Morgan, his wife, and guests came to a landing at the top of some stairs. There, rushing up the stairs at them, was the quite mad Dr. Holt waving two revolvers.

Morgan, who tipped the scales at 220 pounds, pushed his companions aside and hurled himself at Holt. Two shots were fired, wounding Morgan in the hip and groin, but Holt was eventually overpowered and taken into custody. Holt declared that he had no personal animosity toward Morgan. He had attempted to kill the financier in order to focus attention on those obviously annoying munitions sales to the Allied cause.

Holt revealed his dynamite cache in the warehouse. Detectives hurriedly retrieved the trunk. When he admitted sending dynamite to England, ships heading overseas were immediately alerted.

On July 7 a severe explosion took place below decks on the ship Minnehaha, causing a major fire. The vessel was so badly crippled that she was rushed to Halifax, Nova Scotia, the nearest port, where the blaze was extinguished. Dr. Holt had nearly caused a catastrophic disaster. The Minnehaha's cargo was cordite.

In his tiny cell in the Mineola, N.Y. jail, Dr. Holt tried to commit suicide by cutting his wrist with the end of a pencil. After that his cell door was left open, enabling a guard to rush to his aid should there be a further attempt. The next night, when the guard left his station momentarily, Dr. Holt rushed from his cell, climbed the lattice work of the cell block and hurled himself head first to the cement floor below.

The strange mad life of Eric Muenter was over.

JESSIE WAS NO LADY

The area around Boston has always held a particular fascination for me. The towns and villages merge into one another now, but it wasn't always this way. Years ago Peabody, Danvers, and Salem were more definitive in their character and makeup. However, they all had one thing in common – murder.

Even today the name Salem conjures up visions of witch hunts, demons, and executions. In what other town can you have a sandwich in the Witches' Restaurant, then turn a corner and visit the courtroom where the alleged witches were actually sentenced to death hundreds of years ago?

Outside in the bright sunlight of a Massachusett's spring day we are reminded that the Boston Strangler prowled these very towns, seeking victims to satisfy his particular and peculiar desires. But neither witches nor stranglers have brought us to the bustling town of Peabody. The ever-loving wife of Bill Costello is the reason for our visit.

It was a bright but chilly day in Feb. 1933 when Mrs. Costello had occasion to dash upstairs to fetch her purse in order to pay a peddler. The door to door purveyor of fudge almost jumped out of her skin when Mrs. Costello let out a bloodcurdling scream. It was the dear lady's method of letting Peabody, Massachusetts, and indeed all of America, know that she had discovered her husband Bill dead on their bedroom floor.

The discovery of Mr. Costello in this embarrassing state was something of a shock. You see, Bill, whose official title was Captain Costello of the Peabody Fire Department, was a jolly, robust gentleman who only the day before had been in the pink of condition.

An autopsy revealed that somewhere, somehow, Bill had ingested a very substantial quantity of potassium cyanide. When authorities discovered that Mrs. Costello had purchased the very same product only the day before, they became downright suspicious.

But Mrs. Costello had a ready explanation. Before the era of today's modern conveniences many kitchens were equipped with hot water boilers. Most women did their best to blend their boilers into the decor of their kitchen. Many were painted the same shade as the rest of the kitchen. Others were left in their natural metallic state and shined so that you could see your face in them. Mrs. Costello's boiler was of the latter variety. She had purchased potassium cyanide together with Oxalic acid. She didn't consider her purchases poisonous at all. They were to be used to shine up her boiler and that was that. Unfortunately, the police didn't exactly agree. Mrs. Costello was arrested and charged with her husband's murder.

Mrs. Costello's trial lasted through the summer of 1933 and caused a sensation. Bill's widow was a likeable woman who, though ever so slightly overweight, still carried herself with a regal air that belied the fact that she had been a Peabody housewife for many hard long years. Mrs. Costello became the star of the piece.

Two doctors independently took the witness stand and stated that they felt the poison had been administered in capsule form, probably in conjunction with some regular medicine. The medics' testimony was followed by that of a neighbour, Mrs. Bisson, who swore that she had seen her friend Mrs. Costello purchase and fill capsules when caring for a sick friend on a previous occasion. Mrs. Costello didn't need friends like Mrs. Bisson.

Mrs. Costello's attorney presented her as a faithful loving wife whose only aim in life was to provide a good home and a warm bed for her Bill. It therefore came as a shock when the state of Massachusetts came up with Patrolman McMahon of the Peabody Police Dept. who informed the world of another side of Mrs. Costello, which had heretofore been a closely guarded secret between himself and Jessie Costello.

The accused has up to now been referred to as Mrs. Costello, but in keeping with the intimacy of the story he was about to tell, Patrolman McMahon referred to her more familiarly as Jessie. It all began while McMahon, who incidentally was a married man, was directing traffic in Peabody. One day Jessie pulled up in her car and picked up the police officer. From them on it was fun and games, which took place in parked cars and down dark lanes.

When Capt. Bill was away fighting fires, Patrolman McMahon was at his home busy lighting fires of quite a different kind with Jessie. When the rather durable patrolman had his appendix removed, Jessie visited him in the hospital each evening. Shame to tell, Jessie once joined her lover under the white sheets of the hospital bed. Despite great discomfort, Patrolman McMahon, stout fellow that he was, performed admirably. There is more and I could go on, but you get the general idea.

Of course, listening to all this in a courtroom was almost too much for Mrs. Costello to stand. She denied every word, and could not for the life of her figure out why this terrible young man was saying such deplorable things about her. She hardly knew him, and every word he uttered was a barefaced lie.

New England juries have always had a soft spot for ladies who commit murder, particularly those who have led rather pious domestic lives. Despite having a super motive, a great opportunity, and the means at hand to murder her husband, Jessie Costello was acquitted.

Mrs. Costello left the courtroom, walking briskly past Patrolman McMahon and out into the clear New England sunshine. Those sitting close to McMahon later reported that Mrs. Costello directed two very unfavourable words to the patrolman as she walked by. Unfortunately, I will have to leave the two words to your imagination. They were not nice.

ONE LOVER
TOO MANY

Just as some horses run faster than others, and some birds fly higher than others, so it is with men; some are better lovers than others.

Walter Lewis Samples ranks right up there with the all-time champs in the amour department. Walt was a quiet bachelor of sixty-nine who lived in South Memphis. As a retired civil engineer who owned a few rent-producing properties, he didn't indulge in any excesses, with, of course, one exception – ladies. You might even say his hobby ended up killing him.

On Feb. 27, 1941, our hero's doctor received a phone call to come right over. Walt felt that the pains that had plagued him for the last three days were not your average tummy ache. He told the doctor to hurry. Walt proved to have a natural gift as a prognosticator. He died in hospital two days later.

The severe pains sounded like food poisoning to the medic. The deceased had described his last meal as being a breakfast consisting of bacon, eggs, toast, and two glasses of milk. He had also mentioned that the milk did not come from his regular dairy. A different company had obviously left a free sample on the front porch in an effort to gain new business. Fortunately, the half-filled quart of milk was still in

199

the refrigerator. The doctor took one sniff and sealed the bottle. It smelled of phosphorous.

After Walt's death the milk was analyzed, and sure enough, it contained phosphorous crystals and starch, the main ingredients used in the manufacture of rat poison. An autopsy revealed that Walt had indeed been poisoned.

Police investigating the murder were surprised to find scores of letters and photographs in Samples' residence. All were from ladies. The letters should have been mailed in asbestos envelopes – they were almost too hot to handle, describing intimate relations the senders had had with Walt. Some begged to renew old dalliances which, for some reason or other had smouldered and died. Others contained pictures of the ladies in various stages of undress.

All of a sudden the Memphis sleuths had more suspects than enough. Each woman was questioned in the strictest confidence, for several had husbands. Without exception they all claimed that Walt was a terrific lover. Many couldn't wait for his calls, but all professed that they had had nothing to do with his murder. The investigation wound down.

Police meticulously checked back into the records to see if Walt had ever been in any trouble with the law. The best they could come up with was that he had once been the defendant in a minor suit involving a washing machine. A man named LeRoy House had brought the suit against him in order to get back a washing machine his wife had given Walt. Investigation also revealed that House had owned a prosperous trucking firm in Memphis, but had recently sold out and purchased a plantation in Mississippi, a hundred and fifty miles away. The police interviewed a former bookkeeper of the trucking firm and found out that House was extremely agitated when he discovered that his wife had dipped into the till to the extent of $7,000 in order to pass the money along to Walt.

When detectives questioned Mr. and Mrs. House they told almost all. Mrs. House admitted having an affair with Walt that lasted for years. She had tried to break off with the older man, but despite her promises to her husband, she found that it was impossible. Finally, House sold his business and moved out of Memphis so his wife could get away from Walt. Both denied killing the aged Casanova.

A search of the Houses' plantation uncovered several milk bottles from the same dairy as the one found in Walt's home containing the poison. Both Mr. and Mrs. House were taken into custody for questioning. While being searched a will signed by Walt Samples was found in Mrs. House's shoe. The will left everything Walt owned to Mrs. House. Unfortunately, the signature on the will was a forgery.

With the bloodhounds closing in, Mr. House confessed that he had placed the poisoned milk on Walt's porch. His confession completely exonerated his wife. Nevertheless, both Mr. and Mrs. House were placed on trial for first degree murder in June 1941. Both were found guilty and sentenced to twenty years' imprisonment. The couple appealed, and the state Supreme Court ordered a new trial.

During the second day of their second trial, Mrs. House got up from her seat and rushed toward the presiding judge. She shouted, "I can't stand it any longer. My husband is innocent. I did it alone and he's been trying to protect me."

The courtroom was cleared and the true and final story was told. Mrs. House confessed. She knew of Samples' habit of drinking milk at breakfast, and had planted the poisoned milk bottle on the porch. Despite attempting to be faithful to her husband, she could not resist Walt, who seemed to have an unnatural hold on her. In order to free herself she had killed him. What the heck, she figured, the whole thing might as well pay. That's why she forged Walt's signature on a will that she had typed.

House broke down and admitted that he had confessed to the crime to try to save his wife. He had had nothing to do with it. Mrs. House was convicted of murder and again received twenty years. The charges against her husband were dismissed.

THE DEVIL MADE
HER DO IT

Those individuals who inhabit rural environs must, of necessity, furnish their own entertainment. Life on the farm may have an abundance of fresh air, but it does lack those cultural amenities so near and dear to city dwellers.

This humble chronicle involves the murderous career of an agrarian lady who amused herself by attending certain special events. Would you believe funerals?

Martha Hasel had the misfortune to be the only daughter of four children born to poor farmers in the tiny village of Hardscrabble in northern Ohio. By the time she had seen twenty-four summers come and go she was a true woman of the soil.

As the only girl in the family she worked hard. I mean hard. From dawn to dusk she milked cows, cleaned out barns, cooked meals, and patched the menfolk's clothing.

Despite her laborious existence we must never for a moment believe that thoughts decidedly more sensual didn't occupy Martha's imagination. Of course they did. Oftimes as she performed her farm chores her mind dwelt on the gentle caresses of the opposite sex. But Martha had problems. She was much too thin; she was tight-lipped, and had piercing eyes. Martha had never been in the company of a man.

In the spring of 1906 all this changed. Martha attended a box supper. For those of you not acquainted with this social event, let me explain. The eligible females of a rural community would cook a meal, pack it in a box, and have it auctioned off to the highest bidder. This ritual was usually performed in a picniclike atmosphere to raise funds for the local church. The anxious male bidders didn't know whose dinner they were purchasing until they were the proud owner. The successful bidder not only purchased his dinner, he also acquired the company of the female donor.

Albert Wise, a weatherbeaten farmer twenty years Martha's senior, bought her box supper. He walked her home. They courted. They married. Martha moved from working like a dog on her family's farm to working like a dog on Albert's forty acres. She took time off to give birth in quick succession to Kenneth, Lester, Everett, and Gertrude.

It was a hard life, but a good one. Martha was a devoted mother and wife. Eventually she and Albert even managed to pay off the mortgage on their farm. When Martha was forty, and had been married for sixteen years, Albert died from natural causes.

Martha decked out the children in black for the funeral. She laid out Albert, as well as her very best preserves for her guests. Neighbours came from far and wide. Many remarked that her tea biscuits were the tastiest they had ever had. All in all, Martha enjoyed herself tremendously.

Life is for living. Before long Martha's piercing but roving eyes noticed that a city slicker named Walter Johns had purchased the adjoining farm. Martha sent her daughter Gertrude over with an apple pie. It seemed like the neighbourly thing to do.

Walter showed up that very evening to thank the widow Wise in person. Martha was pleasantly surprised. Her new neighbour was a fine cut of a man, not yet forty. Those smouldering embers, which had not even flickered since Albert was laid to rest, now danced merrily within the flat chest of Martha Wise.

Before the crops were harvested that fall, Martha and Walter were frolicking in his house, or in her house, or in the hay, or wherever. It is hard to keep a secret down on the farm. Soon the good folks around Hardscrabble spread the word. The widow Wise and that new man, Walter Johns, were carrying on.

Well, folks, it got so bad that Martha's aged mother, Sophie, decided to have a heart to heart chat with her daughter. The talk didn't do one iota of good. Martha figured that all the gossip would stop the day Walter consented to marry her. Meanwhile, Walter proved a hard nut to crack. He found the current situation very pleasant and had no intention of changing it.

Lily and Fred Geinke, Martha's uncle and aunt, lived just down the road from Martha's farm. They decided to talk to Martha. It did no good. Having assorted relatives nagging her had become a decided bore.

On Dec. 11, 1924, Mrs. Sophie Hasel suffered from extreme stomach cramps. Two days later she was dead.

With Christmas just around the corner, the funeral fitted Martha's social calendar perfectly. Everyone wore black. Martha dabbed at the corner of her eyes as her mother was gently placed under God's good earth. Afterwards, she served her very best preserves and piping hot tea biscuits. All had a rather jolly time that night in Hardscrabble.

Just over two weeks later, on New Year's day, Martha visited her Aunt Lily. The two women discussed their great loss. Both cried, although Martha did mention that the funeral was a great success. She departed after wishing all the family a happy New Year.

That afternoon the entire Geinke family was seized with dry throats, vomiting, and stomach pains. They did the only logical thing. They sent for Martha.

That angel of mercy nursed everyone as best she could. Her best wasn't good enough. Her uncle Fred was buried on Feb. 3. Martha provided food and comfort at her home.

Three days after the funeral Aunt Lily gave up the ghost. Fred's grave was reopened so that Lily could rest by his side forever. Martha cried at graveside. She recovered sufficiently to put up a fine spread of tea biscuits and preserves for friends and neighbours. It should be noted that Martha added ginger cookies and a nutmeg cake for Aunt Lily. No question about it – Martha had become the finest funeral caterer in northern Ohio.

The mysterious illness that had carried away Uncle Fred and Aunt Lily continued to ravish the Geinke children. Marie, Fred, Rudolph, Herman, Richard, and Walter were all rushed to hospital. All recovered. Up to now no one even remotely suspected foul play. However, with the close call suffered by the children, tongues began to wag, resulting in police inquiries.

The county prosecutor thought the deaths suspicious enough to have the body of Lily Geinke exhumed. It was found to contain enough arsenic to kill twenty people. Utensils at the Geinke home were examined. Arsenic was found in the dregs of a coffee pot Martha had used to serve one of the children before he had taken ill.

Once word of the investigation spread throughout the rural area, other people came forward complaining that they too had taken ill after lecturing to Martha about her affair with Walter Johns.

Martha was taken to the town of Medina, where she was questioned extensively by the police. After hours of denying her guilt, she suddenly shrieked, "Yes, I did it. But it was the devil who told me to do it. He came to me while I was in the kitchen baking bread. He came to me while I worked in the fields. He followed me everywhere. It was the devil, I tell you." Martha elaborated, "I poisoned Mom because she laughed at me for falling in love at my age and I poisoned the Geinkes because they made fun of me."

Martha stood trial for her crimes in May 1925. It was revealed that she had killed three people and poisoned seventeen other relatives, who became ill but fortunately recovered. She was found guilty and sentenced to life imprisonment. Martha Wise died a few years later in prison.

PART NINE
THE DOCTORS

DEMEROL WAS DEADLY

To all outward appearances Dr. Charles Friedgood had the world by the tail. A successful surgeon, he owned a large eighteen-room home in the affluent Kensington section of Long Island's North Shore, was the father of a grown, well-educated family, and above all was the husband of Sophie, his loving wife of twenty-eight years.

It just wasn't that way at all. Dr. Friedgood, who was in his mid-fifties, neglected his wife. He arrived home late for meals, sometimes by hours. No matter what the occasion, Sophie never started a meal without him. She waited, and when he finally arrived, she argued, she screamed, and she bickered. To make matters more frustrating, Friedgood ignored his wife's outbursts, and never offered any excuses for his tardiness.

In 1967 Friedgood became infatuated with his Danish nurse, Harriet Larson. Although Harriet wasn't a beauty, she was attractive. Initially the doctor kept his relationship with Harriet a secret, but soon he was carrying on an open affair. For years his daughters, Toba, Esther, Beth, and Debbie had believed that Harriet was nothing more than a faithful employee. Gradually the truth became known to them. Typically, Sophie was the last member of the family to accept the fact that her husband was keeping another woman.

All semblance of secrecy crumbled when Harriet became pregnant. Early in 1972 she flew to Denmark, where she gave

birth to a boy, who was named Heinrich after Dr. Friedgood's dead father. When she came back to the U.S., Friedgood set Harriet and Heinrich up in an apartment not far
from his home. He paid her an allowance of $1,000 a month.
Two years later Harriet found herself pregnant once more.
Again she returned to her native country. This time she gave
birth to a girl, Matte, with Friedgood at her side. He had told
his wife that he was attending a medical convention in Arizona, when in reality he flew to Denmark.

When Harriet and the two children returned to the U.S.,
Friedgood obtained a larger apartment for his second family,
again quite close to his home in Kensington. He helped
furnish it with older pieces from his own home that Sophie
had discarded. Friedgood was under pressure from Harriet
to obtain a divorce from Sophie. He convinced his mistress
that because of financial difficulties incurred while he was
purchasing a hotel, he had signed over everything he owned
to Sophie, almost a million dollars in stocks, bonds, and cash.
As soon as the deal cleared the courts, he would be free to
marry, but in the meantime Sophie legally owned everything.

At the same time the doctor tried to explain away Harriet
to his wife by telling her that he couldn't dismiss his nurse
because she had been witness to several documents he had
signed concerning the same financial deal.

As the Friedgood girls grew up they came to know and like
their father's nurse. Sometimes they were puzzled when little
Heinrich would hug their father and call him Papa. Later
they realized that the child was named after their own grand-
father, and that besides, he bore a striking resemblance to one
of their brothers. One by one the Friedgood girls married.
Each of their husbands eventually learned of the strange,
rather open, relationship their father-in-law had with his
nurse. Occasionally one of his daughters would approach her
father and beg him to explain his relationship with Harriet.
Friedgood wouldn't hear of such scandalous talk. He assured
them that it was nothing more than that of doctor-nurse. He
was so convincing that sometimes his children believed him.

Naturally, Sophie, who over the years had been humiliated

by her husband literally hundreds of times, fought back in the only way she knew. She screamed at him, "Go to your whore!" "Sneak away to your bitch." Friedgood had the exasperating habit of calmly reading his newspaper during these tirades.

The tense relationship between Charles and Sophie Friedgood could not continue indefinitely. Things came to a head on June 17, 1975. That evening Charles and Sophie had a date to meet for dinner at Lundys Restaurant in Brooklyn. Sophie was in good spirits, having heard that Harriet was in Denmark. She arrived promptly at 6 p.m. Typically, Friedgood was late. Sophie sipped wine as she waited for him for over an hour.

After dinner, at approximately 8 p.m., the couple drove in separate cars to their accountant's home, where they were expected. They arrived at 8:30, stayed one hour, and then drove home. At 11 p.m. Esther called her parents from New Jersey. It was an exciting time for her. She and her husband had both just received their law degrees. Esther had a good chat with her mother and father. Moments later Charles and Sophie retired to their bedroom. They were alone in the big house.

We will never know exactly what happened in the Friedgood bedroom after 11 p.m. that night. Later, at Dr. Friedgood's trial, a medical examiner reconstructed the events as they must have unfolded.

Sophie and Charles undressed. Sophie lay in bed while Charles went to a filing cabinet in his study. From the top drawer of the filing cabinet he removed a long needle and syringe. He then filled the syringe with demerol.

Sophie, lying on her back in bed, had no way of knowing she had only moments to live. Charles pounced on his wife, firmly grasping one outstretched arm above her head. As Sophie struggled, Charles injected the demerol up under her armpit. The doctor then held his wife helpless for the ten or twelve minutes it took the demerol to take effect. Sophie screamed frantically. The big house was empty. There was no one to hear.

A few minutes passed. Sophie became drowsy. Her efforts grew weaker. Charles lifted his wife's other arm, and once more jabbed the needle under her armpit. Injections in her thigh and buttocks followed. She lay quiet, but was still breathing. Charles turned his wife's limp form over. He gave her one last injection between the ribs directly into the liver. Sophie stopped breathing.

Dr. Friedgood replaced the needle and syringe in the top drawer of his filing cabinet and returned to his bedroom. He went to sleep beside the lifeless body of the woman who had been his wife for so many years.

Next morning Dr. Friedgood went to work as usual. Lydia Fernandez showed up for work at the Friedgood residence as she did every day. She tidied up around the house, and found it a bit strange that Mrs. Friedgood had not left her a note telling her when she should be awakened. Later that day, at 1 p.m., Lydia found Sophie Friedgood dead in her bed.

Dr. Friedgood was notified of his wife's death. He hurried home. He told of Esther's call the night before, of going to sleep, of waking up, of Sophie kissing him goodbye. It was shocking. His wife must have had a stroke after he left her. Because Sophie had suffered a stroke years before, it was assumed that she had suffered another one.

In keeping with the Friedgood's religion, steps were quickly taken to have Sophie buried in her hometown of Hazleton, Pennsylvania, the following day. Dr. Friedgood signed his wife's death certificate.

News of Sophie's death spread throughout Kensington. Something clicked in Police Chief Raymond Sickles' memory. While he didn't know the Friedgoods personally, he recalled that one of the Friedgood daughters had once frantically called him because her mother and father were having a terrible row. When one of his men arrived at the Friedgood residence they found nothing more than the usual family dispute. Sickles learned that Dr. Friedgood had signed his wife's death certificate. Although there was no law preventing a medical doctor from signing a spouse's death certificate, it was unusual. Normally another doctor would have been called upon to sign the certificate.

Sickles decided to inform the Nassau County Police of his suspicions. Officials felt that Dr. Friedgood's actions were so unusual that they consulted Dr. Leslie Lukash, the County Medical Examiner, who agreed that the funeral should be delayed long enough for an autopsy to be performed. Detective Thomas Palladino was dispatched to Hazleton to see to it that the burial did not take place as scheduled.

While he was mourning at the funeral chapel, Dr. Friedgood was first made aware that the police were concerned about the manner of his wife's death. Under threat that a court order would be obtained granting the autopsy, Dr. Friedgood gave his permission to proceed. He had no choice.

A post mortem was performed at St. Joseph's Hospital, while Detective Palladino looked on. Unbelievably, Dr. Friedgood insisted that he be allowed to observe his own wife's autopsy.

The autopsy revealed that at the time of death Sophie's stomach had been full. How could that be? The meal she had eaten the night before at 8 p.m. would have been digested long before 9 a.m. when the doctor left for work. Sophie must have died within six hours of having eaten the meal. Dr. Friedgood must have been lying when he stated his wife returned his parting kiss the morning after she consumed that meal. She was positively dead at that time.

Dark red bruises were found under the armpits, on the thigh, buttocks, and on the chest. Testing indicated that demerol had been injected in each bruised area. A lethal amount had been injected directly into the liver.

Detectives returned to Long Island hoping to find the needle and syringe in the Friedgood home. While detectives searched the first floor rooms, Dr. Friedgood was able to whisper to Esther, "Upstairs! File cabinet – bottle, syringe – top drawer." Esther looked in her father's eyes. The surgeon held her stare. A father was to be obeyed and protected. Esther calmly strolled upstairs to her father's study. From the top drawer of the filing cabinet she extracted two bottles and a syringe and placed them in a paper bag. Trembling, she lifted up her dress and put the death kit inside her underpants.

Back downstairs Esther told her sister Toba her terrible secret. After the detectives left she showed her sister the contents of the paper bag. One of the bottles was marked demerol. The Friedgood children discussed their father's plight and his obvious guilt with their husbands that night. Meanwhile, Esther had hidden the syringe and bottles in an upstairs closet. She revealed their location only to her father. The death kit promptly disappeared from its hiding place.

A few days later Dr. Friedgood forged his wife's signature to documents dated prior to Sophie's death, giving him access to several of her safety deposit boxes. He forged authorization to sell several of her securities as well. In all, he gathered up $600,000 in cash, negotiable bonds, and jewellery. He then called his daughter Debbie and told her that his doctor had advised him to get away for a few days. No amount of questioning could get him to reveal his destination. Debbie's husband, realizing that his father-in-law's mistress was in Denmark, was convinced that Friedgood was about to skip. He called the police.

Teams of detectives manned the phones calling Kennedy Airport, canvassing overseas flights. There was no one named Friedgood, or anyone matching Friedgood's description flying to Denmark, but the airport computers did come up with a Friedgood flying to London.

Just as Dr. Friedgood's plane was about to take off, it was instructed to return to the terminal. Friedgood was taken off the plane. A search of his luggage revealed the $600,000 horde. Dr. Friedgood was arrested and charged with the murder of his wife. At his murder trial, his children testified against him. In Jan. 1977 he was found guilty and received the maximum sentence possible – twenty-five years to life imprisonment.

In 1978 New York State passed a law known as the Dr. Friedgood Bill, making it illegal for doctors to sign death certificates for relatives.

DR. CROSS LOVED
EFFIE

Dr. Philip Cross surveyed his domain from his fine old home in Dripson, Ireland. The doctor had recently retired from the British Army after serving for many years in India. Now in the winter of 1886 the old man could look forward to many peaceful, if not somewhat boring years, with his wife, Laura, his children, and his retirement estate known as Shandy Hill.

It was not a future that promised much excitement, but many men work a lifetime for just such twilight years of contentment. The doctor was a gruff, introverted man who apparently tolerated the matronly Mrs. Cross as long as she conveniently stayed out of his way. Then again, the British Army does develop character.

When twenty-one-year-old Effie Skinner joined the staff of Shandy Hill as governess to the Cross children the doctor paid little attention. It is hard to believe the doctor ignored the new governess, for Effie was a peach. Her complexion was unblemished, and when she smiled, two pink dimples appeared on each cheek.

It is unclear exactly when the kindly doctor did take notice of this breath of spring. A smile, a touch, a hidden kiss, who knows? At first the embarrassed Effie rejected the doctor's advances. But old Dr. Phil slowly won Effie to his side both literally and figuratively. Stolen kisses in the hall of Shandy Hill led to more basic acts behind closed doors. Dr. Cross and Effie became lovers.

As was inevitable, Mrs. Cross found out about her husband's dalliance with the hired help. Laura could have become indignant, but instead, she decided to let bygones be bygones. After all, Phil had never before acted in this unfaithful manner. Mrs. Cross did the practical thing. She gave Effie her notice. This may not appear to be a major calamity today, but an unemployed governess without references before the turn of the century could literally end up begging on the street.

To the rescue came Dr. Cross. Effie was understandably grateful for any help. The doctor's proposition was simple enough. He would provide the necessary cash for a flat in Dublin and would visit his paramour at every opportunity. Effie became Dr. Cross' mistress.

This new and convenient arrangement went along famously for several months. There was just one thing. The spry old doctor was in love with Effie and wanted to be with her all the time.

Meanwhile, back home at Shandy Hill, Mrs. Cross began to suffer from the most annoying stomach cramps. Sometimes her distress was so severe as to bring on attacks of vomiting. Phil ministered to his wife for several weeks before bringing in Dr. Godfrey, a cousin and friend of the family, for another opinion. Phil explained to his colleague that Laura was suffering from a slight attack of typhoid fever. Dr. Godfrey examined Mrs. Cross and quickly concurred with the older and more experienced doctor. After all, who would detect typhoid fever if not a former military doctor who had spent years in India?

On May 24, 1887, when the local clergyman Rev. Mr. Hayes called to pay his respects to the ill Mrs. Cross, he was told by the kindly doctor that she had just dropped off to sleep. A most distressing week passed for Mrs. Cross. She suffered greatly from nausea and vomiting. On June 2, the maid, Mary Buckley, was awakened by the frantic doctor. Mrs. Cross had mercifully passed away.

Dr. Cross signed the death certificate without delay. Mrs. Cross was laid to rest two days later. The brief ceremony, conducted at graveside at the ungodly hour of 6 a.m., was thought by some good citizens of Dripson to be decidedly odd. It mattered not what the Dripsonites thought, for Dr. Cross was off to his true love.

Like a man possessed, he gathered up Effie in Dublin and sped to London, where the older gentleman and the twenty-one-year-old governess became man and wife. Dr. Phil and Effie tiptoed through the English countryside on their honeymoon. Back in Ireland news reached Dripson that the doctor had married the former governess, and only two weeks after Mrs. Cross had given up the ghost. A relative wrote Dr. Cross informing him that his friends and neighbours had not taken kindly to his actions. The doctor felt that he had better return to Shandy Hill for appearances' sake.

Once ensconced in his old home, the doctor kept a low profile. But nasty rumours failed to abate. There were those who remembered that Dr. Cross had tended to his wife in her final illness. Then there was the hasty funeral. Bad news travels fast. It wasn't long before Inspector Tyacke of the Royal Irish Constabulary heard the rumours.

The Inspector spoke to the coroner, who felt there was enough monkey business taking place to order an inquest. In conjunction with the inquest Mrs. Cross' body was exhumed. An autopsy indicated that she had never had so much as a touch of typhoid fever. What she did have was a massive quantity of arsenic, accounting for the nausea and vomiting she suffered before death.

Dr. Phil was arrested and charged with the murder of his first wife. He didn't have a chance. The prosecution produced one of those chemists who have a habit of taking the witness stand and pointing at the accused. They usually say, "That's the man I sold the poison to." In Dr. Cross' case the chemist added the word "positively." The motive – Effie – was there for all to see.

On Jan. 10, 1888, Dr. Cross, whose hair, incidentally, had turned chalk white during his confinement, was hanged for the murder of his wife.

MRS. MORELL'S WILL

Dr. John Bodkin Adams, fifty-eight, had practised medicine for over thirty-five years in the resort town of Eastbourne, England. He never married, and lived alone in a large Victorian home with only a housekeeper to care for his needs. The doctor had a lucrative practice and was considered to be a pillar of the community. Yet he was to become the central figure in one of the most sensational murder cases ever to unfold in England.

The doctor's life was to become entwined forever with that of a patient, Mrs. Edith Alice Morell. An elderly lady, Mrs. Morell was visiting her son in Cheshire in June 1948, when she suffered a stroke. Taken to the Cheshire General Hospital, she was in great distress, and was given a quarter grain of morphine each day for the nine days she stayed in hospital. On July 5 she was transferred by ambulance to Eastbourne, where she came under the care of Dr. Adams, who remained her doctor until her death on Nov. 13, 1950, at the age of eighty-one. Mrs. Morell's body was cremated, and that, for all intents and purposes, was that.

Six years passed before any further notice was paid to Mrs. Morell and the manner of her death. In 1956 rumours spread in and around Eastbourne that many of Dr. Adams' patients who had died had left him bequests in their wills. These rumours came to the attention of the authorities and it wasn't long before Scotland Yard dispatched senior investigators to look into Dr. Adams and his medical practice. As a result of their inquiries the doctor was arrested and charged with Mrs. Morell's murder.

The murder case that unfolded captured the imagination of the English-speaking world. While many doctors have stood trial for murder in England, rarely had a doctor been accused of murder while ministering to a patient. In fact, the last such case took place over a hundred years earlier, when the infamous Dr. Palmer of Rugelay was convicted of murder. The Adams trial lasted seventeen days, making it the longest murder trial to take place in England up to that time.

Mrs. Morell's stroke had left her partially paralyzed. Eventually she was able to get around with assistance, but required nurses around the clock. Although the alleged crime was six years old at the time of the trial, the nursing records detailing frequency of injections and quantities of drugs administered were available. All medication, whether injected by the nurses or not, was given under the doctor's instructions.

It was established that Dr. Adams was a beneficiary in Mrs. Morell's will. He stood to gain a prewar Rolls Royce, as well as an amount of silver valued at £275. After Mrs. Morell's death Dr. Adams did, in fact, come into possession of these two items.

From the time Mrs. Morell came under Dr. Adams care she received a quarter grain of morphine and a quarter grain of heroin daily. No doubt she became somewhat addicted to the good feeling these drugs gave her, for generally speaking, Mrs. Morell was an irritable and demanding patient.

During September 1950, when Mrs. Morell had only seven weeks to live, her medication was drastically altered by Dr. Adams. He instructed that she be given increased quantities of both morphine and heroin. Mrs. Morell received ten grains of heroin on Nov. 8, twelve grains on Nov. 9, and eighteen on Nov. 11. On Nov. 12, the day before she died, Mrs. Morell received three and a half grains of heroin and two grains of morphine.

Was Mrs. Morell's dosage of these drugs increased in order

to end her life or was the doctor doing everything possible to alleviate pain for a dying patient? The line is a thin one, which many physicians have to walk. Maybe it was even thinner in 1950 than it is today.

Other pertinent events that occurred during Mrs. Morell's illness came to light. Dr. Adams had known he was in his patient's will. At one point he had gone to Scotland for a vacation and Mrs. Morell, in a fit of anger, changed her will, leaving him nothing. Later Dr. Adams returned to her good graces and was placed back in her will. There is little doubt that Dr. Adams was concerned about his patient's will. He had discussed the matter with Mrs. Morell's lawyer on several occasions, and at one point suggested that the lawyer draw up a new will and get Mrs. Morell's son to agree to it at a later date. Mrs. Morell's lawyer turned down such a shady proposition.

Conversely, there was the matter of the competent nurses who took care of Mrs. Morell during her long illness. Not one of them spoke up or suggested that during her last weeks Mrs. Morell's dosage was too high. Even Dr. Adams' partner, Dr. Harris, who filled in for his colleague while he was in Scotland, continued the regime of morphine and heroin. His explanation was that it is customary, all things being equal, to continue medication as prescribed by the regular doctor.

What could be the doctor's motive for murder? He had a lucrative practice and was well respected. Why would he purposely set out to destroy a partially paralyzed elderly woman who had a limited life expectancy? There were those who believed that Dr. Adams set out to make Mrs. Morell totally dependent on him after he realized that she was addicted to drugs. By abruptly increasing her dosage he intended to influence her in any way he wished concerning her will. It must be remembered that Mrs. Morell was an extremely wealthy woman. When her will was finally pro-bated, her estate amounted to £175,000. A tidy sum today, in 1950 this amounted to a fortune.

Detectives uncovered a form, signed by Dr. Adams, which

had secured Mrs. Morell's cremation. One of the questions of the form was, "Have you, as far as you are aware, any pecuniary interest in the death of the deceased?" The doctor answered in the negative, although it is quite clear that he was aware he would receive the Rolls and the silver under the terms of Mrs. Morell's will. Mrs. Morell was cremated the day after her death.

It took six years before the doctor was asked his reason for lying on the cremation form. His only explanation was that he had not lied from any sinister intent, but only to circumvent red tape and get on with the cremation.

On the day of Dr. Adams' arrest he made a statement that was to haunt him throughout his trial. In response to being advised of his rights he told a Scotland Yard detective, "Murder? Can you prove it was murder?" Not exactly the utterance of an innocent man.

During the Adams trial it was revealed that Mrs. Morell was not in pain while under the doctor's care. Expert medical opinion stated that morphine and heroin should be used only if the patient is suffering agonizing pain. Mrs. Morell was irritable and had trouble sleeping. Other drugs should have been used, and furthermore, Dr. Adams, as a competent physician, would know this. In fact, two expert medical witnesses swore that the dosages prescribed by Dr. Adams were certain to cause death.

Dr. Adams' defence attorneys produced experts of their own, who stated that it is impossible to tell exactly how an eighty-one-year-old partially paralyzed woman died. Remember Mrs. Morell's body had been cremated, so it was impossible to perform an autopsy. The defence doctors claimed that it is quite common for an individual who has suffered one stroke to suffer a second, fatal one. In fact, this was suggested to the jury as an alternative to murder.

This theory was ridiculed by the prosecution and contributed the only levity to an otherwise grim affair. Crown Attorneys likened this second stroke theory to the instance of a man walking on a railroad track and being struck by a train. Is it reasonable to assume he had a heart attack a moment before the train struck, and therefore death was not due to a train accident but to a heart attack?

The crux of the Adams' trial revolved around the definition of murder. Murder is an act in which the intent is to kill, and that does in fact kill. A doctor attending a dying patient is compelled to take those measures necessary to relieve pain and suffering, and if his efforts incidentally shorten life, that is not murder. If he deliberately and knowingly cuts off life, that is murder. In the Adams case it was totally irrelevant if life was shortened by a day or by a year. If the intent to kill was there, it was murder. If a doctor errs in his judgement, and institutes measures that effectively terminate life, that is not murder. Intent was of the essence in the Adams case.

Despite the suspicious circumstances surrounding Dr. Adams and his particular brand of medicine, he received the benefit of reasonable doubt. The jury took only forty-four minutes to find him not guilty.

The trial of Dr. Adams for Mrs. Morell's murder stands alone, and I have tried to relate the salient points of the tedious trial as fairly as possible. However, the reader should know that, at the time, Dr. Adams came under strong suspicion for the deaths of two other patients. In fact, at the preliminary hearing that preceded the Morell trial, it was alleged that Adams murdered two other rich patients, a Mr. and Mrs. Hullett. While Adams was in custody, the bodies of these two suspected victims were exhumed, but as the Crown took no action against Adams in this regard, we can only assume nothing incriminating was found.

After his acquittal of the murder of Mrs. Morell, Dr. Adams was arrested and charged with sixteen counts of forging medical prescriptions and contravention of the Cremation and Dangerous Drugs Acts. He pleaded guilty to fifteen of these charges and was fined £2,400.

As a result of these disclosures, the General Medical Council of England had Dr. Adams' name struck off the Register of Medical Practitioners. John Bodkin Adams never practised medicine in England again.

A GIFT OF DEATH

All her life elderly Mrs. Josephine Barnaby had been cursed with poor timing. Take the occasion of her separation from her rich husband, for example. How was Josephine to know that the dear old gent would give up the ghost shortly after they agreed to disagree?

It was most disappointing, if not downright depressing, when the wealthy clothing manufacturer from Providence, Rhode Island left his estranged wife nothing but an income of $2,500 a year. The rest of his large estate was divided between the couple's two adult daughters.

A woman lacking experience in the devious machinations of the world of finance requires the strong arm of a man to guide her through such stressful times. As luck would have it such a gent was on the scene. Dr. Thatcher Graves, the Barnabys' family doctor, volunteered his not inconsiderable business acumen to assist the widow in obtaining her rightful share of the family fortune.

Under the doctor's guidance, Josephine fought the terms of her late husband's will. The courts agreed with her. She was given a huge settlement, which was deducted from her two daughters' shares. Naturally enough, her two married offspring did not cheer for joy at this decision. Forever after relations between mother and daughters were, to put it mildly, strained.

It saddens me to relate that the good Dr. Graves' intentions were not exactly honourable. A married man himself, he had never before stumbled upon such a golden opportunity. He had been instrumental in garnering a fortune for Mrs. Barnaby, and now all he wanted was his just desserts. It was 1889. Times were tough. Mrs. Barnaby trusted the doctor completely.

Dr. Graves obtained power of attorney from Josephine and immediately began making complicated business deals, which had the desired effect of converting her assets to his name. To facilitate his plans, the doctor found it most convenient to send Josephine away on assorted trips, ostensibly for her health. Initially the trips were a pleasant diversion, but eventually they became a nuisance to Josephine. She would no sooner arrive back in Providence than the doctor would present her with railroad tickets for another jaunt.

Josephine began to have second thoughts. While on one of her interminable trips to California she wrote to Dr. Graves informing him that it was her intention to change her will. Josephine received a reply from the kindly doctor advising her in no uncertain terms that she had better smarten up or, as her doctor, he would have her adjudged incompetent. If this step was taken, the doctor let Josephine know she would be unable to sign cheques, sell property, or do any of those things within the scope of competent widows.

Josephine decided it was time to leave California and head back to Providence. She made a scheduled visit in Denver to spend some time with an old friend, Mrs. Worrell.

One day Mrs. Worrell's son brought home a bottle of whiskey, which had been sent to him as a present. He had no idea who had been so generous. An unsigned note had accompanied the bottle. It read, "Wish you a Happy New Years. Please accept this fine old whiskey from your friend in the woods."

As the bottle was received in April of 1891, the ladies thought the sender a bit tardy for New Year's. They giggled as they poured themselves a couple of slugs. Both women were confined to bed the next day.

223

Josephine lingered in agony for six days before expiring. Mrs. Worrell, who apparently was a daintier sipper than her companion, survived.

Strangely enough, the local coroner refused to perform an autopsy. Only after one of Josephine's daughters offered to pay $1,000 was a post mortem conducted. Josephine's body bore traces of arsenic, as did the remains of the whiskey bottle.

Josephine's daughter had always looked askance at her mother's financial dealings with her doctor. Now she was sure someone had murdered her mother, and she wanted to know who and why. It was at her insistence that Josephine's death was considered to be a murder. Dr. Graves' affairs were investigated, and his plundering of Josephine's assets revealed. He was charged with Josephine Barnaby's murder.

At his trial Dr. Graves spent several days on the witness stand, denying everything pertaining to Josephine's death. Prosecution attorneys brought up embarrassing letters the doctor had written to Josephine threatening to have her adjudged incompetent. All the doctor could do was state that everything he did for Mrs. Barnaby was for her own good.

Dr. Graves nearly jumped out of his skin when the state presented Joe Breslyn as a witness. Joe had quite a story to tell. In November 1890, he was travelling through Boston when a fifty-year-old, well-dressed gentleman approached him in the railway station. The gentleman told him he was unable to write and would appreciate having Joe write a note for him. Joe agreed. The man dictated, "Wish you a Happy New Years. Please accept this fine old whiskey from your friend in the woods."

Joe Breslyn swore from the witness stand that the man who dictated the note was none other than Dr. Thatcher Graves. Handwriting experts verified that the incriminating note was written by Joe.

We must pause here to point out that the note was dictated in November, but not sent until the following April, a matter of over four months. No doubt the doctor had the note written by a stranger to guard against the possibility of having his own handwriting compared to that on the note. Of course he never dreamed that Joe Breslyn would end up in court pointing an accusing finger at him.

Why the long wait in sending the poisoned whiskey? Prosecuting attorneys felt that Mrs. Barnaby no doubt mentioned to the doctor that she would be visiting Mrs. Worrell. Not wanting to send the whiskey directly to his victim, Dr. Graves waited until she had arrived at the Worrells'. He may very well have known that Mrs. Worrell's son was not a drinker and would bring the spiked bottle home.

Dr. Graves was found guilty of murder in the first degree and sentenced to hang. He appealed his conviction on technical grounds and was granted a new trial. While in jail awaiting a trial date Dr. Graves was found dead in bed. He had managed to poison himself with morphine.

MURDER IN THE
SWAMP

Come on down Louisiana way to swamp land, where Cajuns still love to pot 'gators and wash down their jambalaya with a good swig of rotgut bourbon. That's where Ada and Jim Le Boeuf were born, lived, and died.

Ada, an attractive southern girl, was only eighteen when she married Jim in 1907. A big, gruff, quiet man, Jim was easily brought to the boiling point. No one messed around with Jim Le Boeuf. Ada liked that quality, which brought respect from other men. She would eventually grow to fear it.

Jim, who had little formal education, started out as a labourer, but ended up as the manager of the Morgan City Power Plant. For a man with his limited ability, he did rather well for himself. He and Ada had a fine home in Morgan City, their own automobile, life insurance, and four children.

On the surface their marriage appeared to be loving and stable. Below this veneer churned the seeds of discontent. As each year went by Ada slipped further and further into drudgery. She washed, she cleaned, she cooked. She was a good mother, a good wife. But she was still a young woman and desperately longed for something better.

The gruff male quality she had so admired in Jim gradually became boring and even despised. Jim was extremely jealous and his constant suspicions only added to Ada's dislike of her husband and her life. In short, Ada was in a rut.

Jim's life was in direct contrast to Ada's. He loved to hunt and fish and spent all his spare time at these activities. Sometimes he would be gone for days with his closest friend, Dr. Thomas E. Dreher and the doctor's rather crude friend, Jim Beadle.

Dr. Dreher had established his practice over twenty-five years before and was one of the town's leading citizens. He was a married man, with a son studying medicine at Tulane University. A good doctor, Dreher never pressed his patients for payment and often accepted whatever they could afford. Everyone in town loved Dr. Dreher.

Now and then someone might remark that Jim Beadle didn't appear to be a suitable companion for the doctor, but others realized Beadle was an expert shot and there was no one better at handling a small boat. The doctor paid Jim Beadle for his services as a loyal guide.

Morgan City had little to offer the bored Ada Le Boeuf in the way of diversion. Perhaps it was inevitable that she and her husband's best friend, Dr. Dreher, would get together. The opportunities were plentiful. Dreher was the Le Boeufs' family physician. He often visited their home socially and professionally. Ada and the doctor became lovers.

As the years passed there were many in the close-knit community who knew very well that Dr. Dreher was bedding down with his best friend's wife. Of course, Jim Le Boeuf had no idea of his wife's infidelity until someone sent a note to Mrs. Dreher. Poor, timid Mrs. Dreher, who really doesn't enter our story as anything other than a victim of circumstances, paid a visit to Jim Le Boeuf.

Jim saw red. While he couldn't prove the serious accusations that Ada vehemently denied, he managed to make his wife's life miserable. Jim swore that if he ever got even a smidgin of proof, he would kill both his best friend and his wife. Ada didn't doubt it for a minute. Jim didn't go fishing or hunting with the doctor and Jim Beadle anymore.

In 1927 the Mississippi overflowed its banks, resulting in

one of the worst floods on record. Morgan City was hard hit. Only two streets escaped the flood waters. Still, the citizens of Morgan City were accustomed to coping with floods. Soon their boats could be seen darting up one street and down another. Life went on.

Naturally, with Jim's strong suspicions, coupled with the flood, Ada's and Dr. Dreher's opportunities for romance diminished. Ada had one confidante, a Mrs. Noah Hebert, who could be trusted to deliver messages to the doctor.

On July 1, 1927, Ada sent her lover a message. It read: "Jim and me will go boat riding on the lake tonight. I talked to him and I believe he will treat you friendly. So meet me tonight and fix this up friendly and we will be friends. I am tired of living this way hearing Jim say he is going to kill both of us. As ever, Ada."

The note sounds almost innocent, but later there were those who claimed that the language was purposely guarded and that the note was in reality Jim Le Boeuf's death warrant.

That night Dr. Dreher and his friend, Jim Beadle, stepped into their green piroque, a canoe-like boat, and paddled silently into the night.

Ada and Jim hitched two boats to their car and drove over to Ada's sister's home for supper. They would go for a boat ride after they dined. It was a beautiful night. When they went boating the Le Boeufs always used two boats. Ada was an excellent oarswoman.

After supper the piroques were taken down from the car. Ada's sister's home was almost surrounded by flood waters. The two boats were launched into a nearby street. Ada suggested they row over a route known to them both, which would lead to Lake Palourde.

The piroques made their way into the dark night. Slowly houses disappeared from view. The muddy swamp water glistened in the moonlight. The trees hung heavy with Spanish moss. Wild flowers peeked out from the decayed branches of long dead trees. It was a night made for murder. Ada carefully led her husband to his death.

The Le Boeufs paddled silently. Gradually they discerned the outline of two men in a boat directly in their path. One of the men shouted, "Is that you, Jim?" "Yes, who's that?" Jim replied.

A shotgun flashed twice, the noise of the reports roaring across the water. Ada turned quickly and rowed away. Jim Le Boeuf would torment her no more. He lay dead in his boat.

Quickly two sixty-five-pound railway angle irons were tied to the body. A knife glistened and in an instant the dead man's stomach was slit open. The body was dumped overboard, the boat sunk, and the two shadowy figures rowed away.

Next morning Ada told her children that she and their father had had a terrible quarrel the night before and he had left. No doubt he would be back when he cooled off.

Six days later some men were hunting alligators on Lake Palourde. They found Jim Le Boeuf's body lying face down under a few inches of water. The heavily weighted body had been prevented from sinking by a small submerged tree.

Ada immediately came under suspicion. She was questioned for three hours before telling police officers that she and Jim had come across two strangers while out boating. It was too dark to identify them. She saw a flash, saw her husband fall, and then panicking, rowed away. She had not told the truth before because she knew her lover would be suspected.

Dr. Dreher was questioned. When informed of Ada's statement, he too admitted being at the scene of the crime, but claimed that Jim Beadle had committed the murder out of loyalty to him. The third member of the unholy trio, Jim Beadle, also admitted being at the scene, but claimed Dr. Dreher had orchestrated the killing and had fired the fatal shots.

All three suspects were arrested and stood trial for the murder of Jim Le Boeuf on July 25, 1927. The murder, because of its eerie setting and the fact that most of the evidence against the accused had come from their own mouths, became a national sensation. The defence offered little in the way of rebuttal.

All three were found guilty. Jim Beadle was sentenced to life imprisonment. Dr. Thomas Dreher, the best-liked man in Morgan City, and Ada Le Boeuf paid for their crime on the gallows.

PART TEN
POT POURRI

THE NEW ORLEANS AXEMAN

It is rare that the murderous frenzy of one man can hold an entire city in terror. Jack the Ripper did it in London in the autumn of 1888 when he mutilated and murdered five prostitutes. The Boston Strangler, Albert DeSalvo, managed to keep the greater Boston area in a state of fear when he sexually attacked and murdered thirteen women. In recent years David Berkowitz, better known as Son of Sam, kept New York City in a state of near panic as he wounded seven innocent victims and murdered six others.

Another mass murderer, not as well known as the ones mentioned here, may have been the strangest of all. The Axeman of New Orleans first struck in 1911.

A hardworking Italian grocer named Cruti went to sleep above his store and never woke up. During the night someone gained entrance to his living quarters and, using Cruti's own axe, beat his sleeping victim about the head until he lay dead in a pool of his own blood.

Cruti's murder appeared to be an isolated incident until another grocer named Rosetti was murdered in exactly the same manner. Rosetti's wife became the third Axeman victim as she lay sleeping beside her husband.

That same year the Axeman claimed victims number four and five. Tony Schiambra and his wife were cruelly bludgeoned to death with their own axe as they slept. Police scrambled to find the madman who only killed Italian grocers.

As suddenly as the strange killings began, they abruptly stopped. It wasn't until May 23, 1918, seven years later, that the Axeman struck again. On that night Joseph Maggio and his wife went to bed early in the living quarters behind their grocery store. They were never to leave their bedroom alive. During the night someone chiselled a panel out of the back door of their apartment. The madman entered the apartment carrying an axe he had picked up in the Maggios' yard. He proceeded directly to the bathroom where he found Maggio's straight razor. Quietly entering the bedroom, he swung the axe first at Maggio's head and then rained a blow upon the sleeping Mrs. Maggio. He leaned over both his victims and slit their throats. Both bloodstained weapons were found in the backyard where the killer had discarded them.

Initially some suspicion fell on Maggio's two brothers, Andrew and Jake, who lived in the same building. Both were able to prove that they were elsewhere on the night of the attack and were quickly exonerated. Police scanned the records of the old 1911 unsolved murders, but believed that the current axe murders were not connected with the older crimes, despite the similarity of the victims.

A little over a month later, on June 28, a baker, John Zanca, delivered bread to the back door of Louis Bessemer's living quarters behind his grocery store. Just as Zanca was about to leave, Bessemer opened the back door. Blood was streaming down his face from a vicious looking scalp wound. Zanca shouted to Mrs. Bessemer. Receiving no reply he made his way into the bedroom where he found Mrs. Bessemer unconscious on her bloodsoaked bed. Zanca called the hospital and the police. A blood-stained axe was found in the bedroom.

Bessemer was treated at hospital and released. His wife was more seriously injured but still alive. Bessemer could shed little light on the identity of his attacker or the motive. He explained to the authorities that the woman believed to be his wife was in reality a Mrs. Lowe, with whom he had been living for some time.

All Bessemer could tell detectives was that he had received a vicious blow to the head with his own axe. When his head cleared he got out of bed and found Mrs. Lowe moaning on the balcony. He carried her to her bed and was just leaving for help when Zanca showed up at the door.

Mrs. Lowe was able to give authorities their first description of the axe murderer. She had been attacked as she stood on her balcony, and had caught a glimpse of her axe-wielding assailant before being struck. She described him as being white, with dark brown hair, quite tall, and heavy set.

Mrs. Lowe's condition grew steadily worse. Doctors felt that an operation was necessary if she were to have any chance of survival. Unfortunately the operation was not successful, and Mrs. Lowe died on Aug. 5.

That very night the Axeman struck again. Edward Schneider returned to his home to find his pregnant wife lying in a pool of blood in her bedroom. Edward rushed his wife to the hospital, where doctors were able to save her life. She told of waking up to see a shadowy figure lurking over her bed. An axe flashed, and that was all she remembered. A week later this remarkable woman gave birth to a healthy baby girl.

On Aug. 10 the Axeman claimed another victim when he caved in Joseph Romano's head as he slept. By now the residents of New Orleans waited in dread for the Axeman to strike. The Italian community in particular was close to panic. Who could figure out what manner of man was going about in the middle of the night, obviously seeking out Italian grocers to butcher in their sleep?

On March 10, 1919, grocer Charles Cortimiglia, his wife and two-year-old daughter were the recipients of the madman's wild machinations. A competitive grocer on the same street, Iorlando Jordano and his eighteen-year-old son Frank, heard the Cortimiglias' screams from across the street and ran to their aid. They found the two adults soaked in blood from scalp wounds. Mrs. Cortimiglia held her daughter in her arms. The child was dead.

Rushed to hospital, both parents survived. They had seen their attacker and gave general descriptions of the Axeman. Mrs. Cortimiglia amazed detectives when she declared that she knew the killers. They were none other than Iorlando Jordano and his son Frank. She claimed that Frank was the axe-wielding killer.

Mr. Cortimiglia stated that his wife was definitely wrong in her identification of the two Jordanos. Despite this, both men were arrested and charged with murder. The rift between the two Cortimiglias became so heated that they separated over their diametrically opposed identification of the attackers. Mr. Cortimiglia claimed that there had been only one attacker and that his wife must have become insane at the shock of seeing her own daughter murdered.

At the murder trial that followed, Rosie Cortimiglia received much sympathy because of the loss of her daughter. The jury was inclined to believe her rather than her husband. Both Jordanos were found guilty. Frank was sentenced to hang, while his father received life imprisonment. It is hard to fathom the reasons for the Jordanos being brought to trial. Surely all the Axeman's trademarks were evident in Cortimiglia's attack. The door panel had been chiselled; the bloody axe owned by the occupants had been left behind.

Meanwhile there was no let-up in the activities of the Axeman. On Aug. 10 Steve Boca staggered out of his home after being attacked with an axe. He could shed no light on the identity of his assailant. The panel of his back door had been removed by a chisel. Two months later Mike Pepitone and his wife were attacked. Mrs. Pepitone survived, but Mike died from head wounds.

Abruptly the attacks stopped. Mike Pepitone was the Axeman's last victim.

In the interim the Jordanos lawyers had appealed their convictions. Father and son languished in jail. It was now a year and nine months since the night they had gone to the

Cortimiglias' aid only to find themselves convicted of murder.

On Dec. 7, 1920, Rosie Cortimiglia walked into the office of a New Orleans newspaper and blurted out her story. "I lied, I lied! God forgive me, I lied; I hated the Jordanos because they were vicious business competitors, but they did not kill Mary." After the legal necessities were dispensed with, the two Jordanos were released. The only evidence against them had been Rosie's positive identification.

Who was the mad Axeman? Unlike the Jack the Ripper case there is every reason to believe that the murders have been solved in a strange and unusual manner.

On Dec. 20, 1920, a native of New Orleans, Joseph Mumfre, was strolling down a Los Angeles street in broad daylight. Suddenly a woman approached Mumfre, and without saying a word, pointed a revolver at him and didn't stop shooting until the gun was empty.

The woman claimed that Mumfre was the New Orleans Axeman. When New Orleans detectives were contacted, they checked Mumfre's prison record against the dates on which the attacks started and stopped. Sure enough, Mumfre had been at large in 1911 when Cruti, Rosetti, and Schiambra had been attacked. Then he was back in prison for seven years, and was released just before the date of the Maggio attack in 1918. All other lulls in the murderous spree coincided with Mumfre's numerous prison sentences.

Mumfre's killer was charged with murder. During her trial she claimed that she recognized Mumfre and knew he was the New Orleans Axeman. Although she pleaded guilty, her lawyers claimed that the homicide was justified. Mumfre's murderer was found guilty and received a sentence of ten years in prison. She was released after serving only three years.

Her name was Mrs. Mike Pepitone.

WAS IT PADDY?

Despite the many safeguards in our judicial system explicitly designed to protect innocent parties from conviction, is it still possible to be perfectly innocent and be convicted of a major crime? The truth is that the vast majority of persons convicted of major crimes are indeed guilty. It happens rarely that an innocent individual is proven guilty beyond a reasonable doubt. This is the story of one such incident.

Patrick Meehan was a safecracker who operated in and around Glasgow, Scotland all his life. Paddy began his criminal career at the age of ten, when he stole from fruit shops in the poverty-stricken Gorbals district of Glasgow. Although his family was poor they were a hard-working, respectable lot who had never been in trouble with the law. Paddy's two brothers, one older, one younger, grew up in the same circumstances and both became law-abiding citizens.

Paddy attended special schools for uncontrollable youngsters. Once he became an expert safecracker, he was in and out of jail continually. No sooner would he be released from prison than he would be apprehended, convicted, and sent back to serve another sentence. About the best thing one can say about Patrick Meehan is that during his long criminal career he never resorted to physical violence.

After being released from an enforced vacation in Borstal at eighteen, Paddy met and married sixteen-year-old Betty

237

Carson. The marriage was successful after a fashion, but Betty saw little of her husband in the ensuing years. He spent more time in prison than out.

While serving time in 1967 in Parkhurst Prison on the Isle of Wight, Paddy met fellow convict James Griffiths. At the age of six Jimmy was swiping the belongings of other little boys. After a series of special schools, he too graduated to breaking and entering, for which he was sent to prison. In 1965 Griffiths achieved a measure of fame by becoming one of the few men to have escaped from Parkhurst. Three months later he was taken into custody and return to prison. That's when he became acquainted with Paddy Meehan.

After completing seven years at Parkhurst, Paddy returned to Glasgow and was reunited with Betty. Paddy made an attempt to go straight. He tried to find a good-paying job, stayed home nights with Betty and, all things considered, seemed to be making an honest effort to begin a new life.

One day Jimmy Griffiths showed up at the Meehan flat. He had some stolen jewellery he wanted to convert into cash. Paddy obliged by putting him in touch with a dealer. Jimmy, sporting a different stolen car each time he visited, became a frequent guest of the Meehans. By the summer of 1969 Griffiths was living with seventeen-year-old Irene Cameron. He was making his living stealing, specializing in automobiles.

Jimmy Griffiths talked Paddy into casing a safe in Stranraer. The Motor Taxation Office in Stranraer stored car registration books that would enable Jimmy to sell his stolen cars directly rather than through a middle man. Using a stolen Triumph, the two friends took off on a trip that was to change both their lives forever. By 7 p.m. on July 5 they arrived at Stranraer.

* * *

Abe Ross and his wife Rachel lived at 2 Blackburn Place, Ayr. Abe was sixty-seven and Rachel was seventy-two. Abe commuted each day to Glasgow, where he owned and ran a successful Bingo game in Paisley. He worked four nights a week at his Bingo Emporium, arriving home at approximately 11:30 p.m. with his night's proceeds, which he deposited in a safe in his home. Abe and Rachel had been married for thirty-six years. On July 5, a Saturday, Abe passed the evening watching television with his wife. They went to bed around midnight.

A short time later two men entered the Ross' bedroom. Without a word one jumped directly on top of Mrs. Ross, and struck her in the face. The other intruder jumped on Abe, but in the struggle that followed Abe found himself on top of his assailant, who shouted, "Get this ____ off me, Pat." Mrs. Ross' attacker left her for a moment and beat Abe on the head with an iron bar. The two men placed Abe on the floor and threw a blanket over his head. Every time he moved they pounded him with the bar. A large pool of blood surrounded the area around his head. One of the men returned to Rachel Ross and struck her repeatedly with the iron bar. The men then tied the elderly couple's hands behind their backs.

After several more blows to the head Abe revealed the location of his safe. The robbers took out about £3,000. Feeling that it would seem less suspicious if they left the Ross' residence in daylight, they decided to wait several hours until morning. The two men sat down at the kitchen table and proceeded to drink whiskey and lemonade. Abe Ross remained conscious. He thought he heard one of the men say, "They're not here yet, Jimmy."

At about 5:30 a.m. the two men tied the Ross' feet. Rachel begged them to call an ambulance, and one exclaimed, "Shut up, shut up, we'll send an ambulance." Then they left.

Abe Ross and his wife lay in their own blood all day Sunday. Abe had managed to get the blanket off his head, but couldn't undo the ropes that bound his hands and feet. Night fell. Rachel groaned. It wasn't until Monday morning when a servant showed up for work that the Rosses were discovered and taken to hospital. The following day Rachel Ross died. Abe, although seriously injured, recovered.

Paddy Meehan and Jimmy Griffiths had spent their Saturday evening studying the Motor Taxation Office at Stranraer, about fifty miles from the Ross' home in Ayr. Paddy decided that the safecracking job was too risky. Around 1:45 a.m. the pair started back towards Glasgow. At a point just beyond Prestwick Airport they spotted a hitchhiker, pretty Irene Burns. The two men stopped. Irene explained that two boys had picked her up along with her friend, Isabel Smith. When the boys got fresh the girls insisted on getting out of the car. The boys slowed down, let Irene out, and sped away with Isabel. Paddy and Jimmy decided to give chase. They caught up to the other car at Kilmarnock and forced it to stop. Isabel joined Irene, and the two men gave the girls a lift to convenient drop-off points. At approximately 4:30 a.m. Griffiths dropped Paddy off at his flat.

For the next few days the attack on Mr. and Mrs. Ross was front-page news. All known criminals in the Glasgow area were interrogated. Pat Meehan was one of the men questioned. Pat realized he was in a delicate position. His alibi placed him in a stolen car planning a robbery with a known criminal near the scene of the Ross' attack. Despite the risk Paddy decided to tell the truth, including his little adventure with the two young girls. Then he phoned Jimmy Griffiths, telling him what he had done and asking him to come forward in support of his alibi. Jimmy wrestled with his conscience. If he admitted stealing the car it would mean several years back in prison.

Paddy Meehan was arrested and placed in an identification parade. Abe Ross had never actually seen his assailant, but swore he could never forget his voice. As number one in the lineup Paddy Meehan was asked to say the words, "Shut up, shut up, we'll send an ambulance." Abe Ross almost collapsed. He didn't need to hear any other voices. He had just heard the killer. The identification parade was over. The other witnesses were sent home.

Patrick Meehan pleaded that there was one man who could verify his story – Jimmy Griffiths. In the meantime

Griffiths was torn between loyalty to his friend and saving his own skin. He even called the police and told them Paddy was innocent, but refused to turn himself in.

Police located Griffiths' flat at 14 Holyrood Cr. Five unarmed detectives showed up to apprehend Jimmy. It was a mistake. Jimmy opened fire, wounding one man and sending the remaining four scurrying for cover. Police called in reinforcements. In the gun battle that took place, thirteen passersby were wounded, and one killed. Jimmy Griffiths was shot dead with a bullet in his heart. Thus died Paddy Meehan's collaborating witness.

At Paddy's murder trial the prosecution presented a formidable case. The two men in the Ross' home had called themselves Paddy and Jimmy, the same first names as Meehan and Griffiths. Meehan was a known criminal who admitted to being in the vicinity of Ayr on an illegal errand on the night of the murder. Above all, Mr. Ross swore it was Meehan's voice he had heard in his home on the night of the attack.

The homes of Meehan and Griffiths were thoroughly searched and nothing connecting them to the Ross' residence was found. The names Paddy and Jimmy are not uncommon in Glasgow. Would two experienced criminals use their correct names during the commission of a serious crime? Would these same men pick up a hitchhiker immediately after committing a robbery, thereby placing themselves near the scene of the crime?

The jury took only two hours to find Paddy Meehan guilty of murder. He was sentenced to life imprisonment.

Three years later Ian Waddell, a known criminal, approached his lawyer with the idea of confessing to the Ross killing. He had three stipulations. He would only tell his story under the influence of truth serum, so that the prosecution would be unable to use the evidence later to charge him with murder. He would not reveal the identity of his accomplice, and he wanted £30,000 from a T.V. station or a newspaper for his trouble. Ian Waddell met with reporters, who had hidden a tape recorder. He revealed enough intimate details of the interior of the Ross' home to prove that he, and not Paddy Meehan, was the guilty party. No paper or television organization took up Waddell's offer, but the new evidence was turned over to the authorities.

Despite this strong evidence, the Secretary of State ruled that there were no grounds warranting any further action in the case. A year later, in 1975, the elderly Mr. Ross revealed that, looking at all the events in hindsight and considering his distraught condition at the time of his wife's death, it was possible he had picked the wrong man from the voice identification. On May 19, 1976, Patrick Meehan was granted a Royal Pardon and was released from Peterhead Prison.

TONI JO AND
HER COWBOY

This is the saga of two lovers who were wild, reckless, and acted without a thought for anyone else. They lied, stole, and even killed, but they remained loyal, faithful, and above all, deeply in love with each other.

Annie Beatrice McQuiston was born on Jan. 3, 1916, in Shreveport, Louisiana. She was the last of six children whose father was an honest, hard-working railway worker. Tuberculosis took the life of Mrs. McQuiston when Annie was only six. From then on the youngest member of the family was a handful. She hated school and loved a good time. By the time she was fourteen she was a knockout. At sixteen she left home, gravitating from employment as a dance hall hostess to being a full-time prostitute in the red light district of Shreveport.

At twenty-one Annie changed her name to the more glamorous Toni Jo. She was an alcoholic, who quickly graduated to drugs. Police were familiar with the young prostitute, and had arrested her for drug violations and prostitution six times before her twenty-second birthday.

Claude D. (Cowboy) Henry had been a professional heavyweight boxer. He was a big, well-built man, well over six feet. Cowboy didn't have too much going for him, and had been in and out of minor scrapes all his life. He was in a serious predicament when he met Toni Jo. While hoisting a few in a bar in San Antonio, Texas, he got into an argument that turned into a fight. During the fight a San Antonio police officer was killed. Cowboy was charged with murder and was convicted, but the verdict had been set aside. He was successful in obtaining bail and was released to await his second trial for the murder of the police officer.

The pair met in 1939. It was love at first sight. Toni Jo, wise in superficial affairs of the heart, fell genuinely in love with Henry. The big ex-boxer worshipped the ground Toni Jo walked on.

Well aware of Toni Jo's profession and lifestyle, Henry decided to take things one at a time. With Henry's encouragement, Toni Jo decided to kick the drug habit. She quit cold turkey, and with Henry at her side for the following three agonizing months, she was successful. Toni Jo and Henry were married in Sulphur, Louisiana.

It might have been possible for them to pull it all together if they had been able to start over with a clean slate. Unfortunately, life doesn't work that way. Henry stood trial for the murder of the police officer for the second time. Again he was found guilty. He was sentenced to fifty years in prison at Huntsville.

Toni Jo was shattered. Just when she had some hope of a future, it was gone. From the day the jury handed down their verdict, she swore she would get her man out of jail.

As a first step she moved to Beaumont to be closer to the prison. Then she sought out former inmates who might have connections within the prison. That's how she met an ex-con called "Arkansas." He listened intently as Toni Jo told him she would do anything to get Henry out. Arkansas agreed that it could be done, but only if she followed his advice.

The plan was to first get guns, then money, and finally to make enough connections inside the prison to facilitate the escape. On Feb. 13, 1940, Arkansas and Toni Jo were successful in hiring two teenage boys, who managed to steal sixteen revolvers from a hardware store in Beaumont.

The next step was to hold up a bank. Arkansas said he had

already cased one that should be easy pickings, but they needed a fast, new car. On Valentine's Day the pair posed as hitchhikers. Joseph Calloway, driving a late model vehicle, pulled over to the curb. Toni Jo and Arkansas jumped in. They had only gone a short way when Toni Jo stuck a revolver in Calloway's side and ordered him out of the car and into the trunk. Arkansas took over the wheel.

He drove for a while, then pulled up. Arkansas wanted to know what Toni Jo had in mind for the man in the trunk. Without a word, Toni Jo got out of the car, opened the trunk, and marched Calloway across a ploughed field to a haystack. Holding a .32 calibre revolver on her captive, she ordered Calloway to undress. There, on the isolated southern farm, the strange love-crazed former prostitute suggested that her captive pray. Calloway knelt in the mud. While he prayed Toni Jo shot him squarely between the eyes.

When she returned to the waiting Arkansas, he inquired about the shot. Toni Jo told him that she had killed Calloway to silence him forever. Arkansas suddenly had new respect and fear for his travelling companion. That same evening the desperate pair checked into a hotel. A short time later Arkansas sneaked out of the hotel and took off with the stolen car.

Three days later Toni Jo appeared at the home of her aunt who lived near Shreveport. She hadn't seen nor corresponded with this aunt for years, yet she told her the entire story of her love for Cowboy Henry. She also told her that she had killed a man who had given her a lift in his car. Toni Jo's aunt called the police. The former prostitute had a hard time convincing them that her story was true, but when they checked and found that a man named Calloway was missing, they knew they had something.

Toni Jo led the police to Calloway's body. She then gave the police officers the murder weapon and the dead man's wallet, but she wouldn't divulge any information about her accomplice, the mysterious Arkansas.

In the meantime, Calloway's car turned up abandoned in Arkadelphia, Arkansas. Police agreed to transport Henry from Huntsville to Beaumont in return for his promise to use his influence to persuade Toni Jo to give police the information they wanted.

Their five-minute private meeting proved successful. Toni Jo told the officers that Arkansas' real name was Harold Burks. The F.B.I. soon traced Burks to the home of a relative in Warren, Arkansas. He was arrested and confessed to his part in the crime.

Then Toni Jo pulled the rug out from under the entire case. She now stated that her story was completely fabricated. She swore that at no time did she ever get out of the car. She claimed that Burks led the man into the field and shot him.

For his part, Burks stated that he had had no intention of going all the way with Toni Jo's scheme to get her man out of prison. He merely thought he would have better luck hitch-hiking with an attractive girl. As things turned out, the day he met Toni Jo was the unluckiest day of his life.

Toni Jo and Burks were charged with first degree murder. During her trial Toni Jo insisted that Burks was the actual killer. Despite this she was convicted and sentenced to die. She appealed twice, and each time was granted a new trial. On both occasions the result was the same. She was convicted and sentenced to death.

Burks was also convicted of first degree murder, claiming that Toni Jo was the murderer. He too received the death sentence.

As her execution date of Nov. 28, 1942 drew near, Toni Jo had a change of heart. With only eight days to live she confessed that her original story was correct in every detail. She had indeed pulled the trigger and acted alone in killing Calloway. She was now telling the truth because she knew nothing could save her, and she didn't want Burks' execution on her conscience.

Once again the entire case took a dramatic turn. Cowboy Henry escaped from prison by crashing through the prison gates in a truck that was later found abandoned six miles from the prison. Henry swore that he would take a hostage whom he would kill if Toni Jo were not released from death row. Everyone concerned took his threat seriously.

Huge spotlights were installed around the St. Charles Jail, which housed Toni Jo. Guards were posted around the clock. Extra state troopers patrolled the highways. Judges and lawyers who had taken part in Toni Jo's three trials were guarded night and day.

A few days later, an underworld informant told the police where to locate the wanted man. He was picked up in a Beaumont hotel and surrendered quietly.

Henry begged to be allowed one last phone call to his wife. Permission was refused. Toni Jo pleaded for a few moments on the phone with Henry. Twenty-four hours prior to her date with death Toni Jo was brought to the warden's office, where she received a call from the Huntsville prison. It was her husband, Cowboy Henry. The pair expressed their love for each other. The next day Toni Jo was executed in the electric chair.

In March 1943, Harold Burks was executed for the same crime.

TRY, TRY AGAIN

A.D. Payne and his wife Eva had been married fifteen years when A.D. decided to kill her. Eva Payne, who had once been a lovely young student at West Texas State Teachers College, was now forty, and had "let herself go."

Lawyer A.D.'s secretary, Olive Taylor, on the other hand, was a mere babe of twenty-one. Innocent blue eyes blinked provocatively as she sat there with dainty legs crossed, steno pad at the ready, while A.D. dictated some boring contract.

When spring came to Amarillo, Texas, in 1928, A.D. thought to himself, "The hell with Eva and the two children at home." He blurted out his true feelings to Olive in the middle of dictation. Somewhat embarrassed, but receptive to a point, Olive explained that while she was attracted to him she had her own code of ethics. No hanky panky before she was married, and certainly never with a married man. A.D. was shattered, but didn't stop trying. Sometimes A.D. pleaded with Olive right in the office. Olive pretended not to hear, and just jotted down what he said in her notes.

A.D. decided that something had to give. He placed $10,000 insurance on Eva's life, with a double indemnity clause included in case Eva met her death by accidental means.

A.D. and Eva slept in adjoining bedrooms equipped with both electricity and gas jets. Eva often forgot to turn off the gas when she heated her hair curlers. Circumstances were made to order for A.D. One cold winter night he waited until Eva was sound asleep before turning on the gas. Then he crawled back into his bed. A while later the Payne's eight-year-old son staggered into A.D.'s room shouting, "Daddy, I smell gas!" There was nothing else Daddy could do. Pretending to react to the emergency he rushed to Eva's aid. She was unconscious but A.D. managed to revive her, with his son looking on. Eva sobbed out her appreciation, all the while promising she would never forget to turn off the gas jets again.

Two months later A.D.'s wife was bedridden with the flu. As she wheezed and coughed our hero calmly dissolved eight morphine tablets in a glass of water and forced his wife to drink the concoction so that she would never return to her nagging ways again.

Within minutes Eva's pulse became weaker; she slumped into unconsciousness. A.D. went to his office. That evening he returned home, expecting his wife to be dead. Instead he found her sleeping peacefully. When Eva awoke in the middle of the night she remarked how very strong the medicine had been. It had been a long time since she had slept so soundly. A.D. stared at the ceiling and clenched his fists in anger. Just wait till next time, he thought.

Next time wasn't long in coming. A.D. and Eva went for a drive in the family auto. The scheming lawyer decided to park on a steep hill facing Bishop's Lake to look at the view. Because of the sharp incline A.D. put on the emergency brakes. Being a cautious soul he informed his wife that he better place a few large rocks under the rear wheels. One couldn't be too careful, you know. He returned to the car, but it wasn't long before A.D. decided that he'd better take a look at the rocks to see if they were holding properly. This time he sneakily released the emergency brake before getting out of the car. With a broad smile, A.D. kicked the boulders from under the car's rear tires. Nothing happened. In desperation he got behind the car and pushed. Just as he thought he might be making headway, a car drove up and parked directly behind his vehicle. A.D. was forced to drive away without accomplishing his mission.

This time nothing would save Eva. Late one night A.D. rigged up a black thread between the trigger of a shotgun and the door of Eva's broom closet. When Eva opened the door the blast would certainly blow her head off.

Next morning the children left for school. A.D. read the morning paper. Eva began her housework. She opened the closet and the shotgun roared. A couple of pellets entered Eva's right hand. The contraption had fired wide and low. A.D. solicitously washed the blood from the superficial wound, promising to be more careful with his shotgun in the future. Then he went downstairs and destroyed the black thread.

A.D. obviously believed in the old adage, "If at first you don't succeed, try, try again." He decided he would park his car on a railway crossing while Eva slept in the front seat, which she had the habit of doing, particularly after a good meal and a couple of drinks. A.D. took Eva out for an evening on the town. On the return trip home Eva fell asleep. Everything was perfect this time. About two miles from the railway crossing A.D. ran out of gas.

Are you keeping track? This is attempt number six coming up. When Eva took a bath it was her custom to set up an electric heater on a little shelf above the tub. A.D. decided that the next time Eva bathed he would hang up a picture on the wall behind the little shelf. As he hammered away the heater would slide off the shelf into the tub, electrocuting the unsuspecting Eva. All went as planned. Eva splashed playfully in the tub. A.D. hammered on the outside wall. Nothing happened. A.D. peeked into the bathroom to see what had gone wrong. Eva had innocently taken the heater from the shelf and placed it on the floor.

Would our hero call it a day? No, he would try again. This time he called his own office several times, disguising his voice and threatening to kill A.D. Payne. Now he figured he had established a reason to plant a bomb in his own car, which, of course, would blow up Eva. On June 27, 1929 Eva Payne was graciously given the use of the family car for the day. After a full year of trying to kill his wife, A.D. succeeded. Eva was blow to smithereens. When police notified A.D. he was beside himself with grief.

The bungling lawyer almost got away with murder. An industrious reporter, Gene Howe of the Amarillo *Globe*, received permission to go through all A.D.'s office records and notes, figuring that he might uncover an enemy who could have wanted to kill the lawyer. When young Howe read Olive's shorthand dictation notes, he realized immediately that he had indeed uncovered a motive for murder.

Olive Taylor was questioned. She told of A.D.'s love. It was only a hop, skip, and jump to the insurance company with its potential $20,000 payoff. Police then located a construction company in San Antonio that had sold A.D. dynamite.

A.D. was taken into custody. A day later he confessed to the District Attorney. It is his story that is related here, for no one other than A.D. knew of his many attempts on his wife's life. A few days after confessing to murder A.D. made another bomb in jail. No one has ever been able to figure out how he had the materials smuggled into his jail cell.

A.D. Payne was successful on his very first attempt to blow himself up.

FORTUNATELY FOR SPOSATO

Take one fortune teller, a conscientious lawyer, and a dead man, mix well, and presto, you will come up with a murder case with a difference. This tale took place at the turn of the century when Denver, Colorado was an expanding metropolis of 100,000 souls, all intent on making an honest or dishonest buck, whichever came first. The city boasted a mixture of several ethnic groups, not the least of which was Italian.

It all happened so fast it was hard to believe that a life had been snuffed out in less time than it takes to blink an eye. John Brindisi told the police his story. Frank Lotito wasn't talking. He was lying face down in the gutter with a .38 slug in the back of his neck.

Brindisi and his brother-in-law Lotito were knocking back a few in a saloon when Frank Sposato joined them. For no apparent reason Sposato tried to pick a fight with the two men. Deciding that caution was the better part of valour, they left the saloon. Sposato followed them outside and shot twice at Brindisi, missing him both times. He then aimed at Lotito and didn't miss. Brindisi swore that he and his brother-in-law had been unarmed.

While this little narrative was being related to the Denver cops, Frank Sposato was a few yards away, leaning against a lamp post. A crowd of men had encircled him. There was real danger that Frank would be lynched then and there. Sensing

252

the mood of the mob, three police broke through the crowd and approached Sposato. They asked him for his gun. Without saying a word, Frank turned over an Iver-Johnson .38 hammerless. The cops hustled Sposato into a patrol wagon and down to the police station.

The following day, March 4, 1901, thirty-four-year-old Horace Hawkins heard of the drama. Horace was a lawyer on the way up, and knew the accused man well. Frank Sposato was an official court interpreter in the predominantly Italian west side. Horace couldn't believe that the handsome, well-bred Sposato could shoot someone in cold blood. Horace became Sposato's lawyer. To say that things looked bad for his client was an understatement; the situation looked hopeless.

Lotito had been shot in the back of the head. The victim was unarmed. Several witnesses had seen the men quarrelling in the saloon. Brindisi swore that he had witnessed the shooting. Then there was the Iver-Johnson with its three discharged shells.

Sposato's story was different. He told Horace that he had stepped into the saloon for a beer. He was not acquainted with either Lotito or Brindisi. They entered the saloon and took up positions on either side of him at the bar. The two men started elbowing and shoving him back and forth. He warned them to stop, but when they didn't he punched Lotito in the face. The bartender intervened and ordered all three men off the premises.

Sposato lingered until his tormentors left. Then he too went outside. Lotito and Brindisi jumped him, but he fought them off. They ran into the shadows between two buildings. Suddenly one of them took a shot at him. Sposato claimed that he ducked behind a lamp post and fired twice in self-defence toward the shadows. Horace believed that his client was telling the truth. Why were there three discharged shells in Sposato's revolver when he swore he had only shot twice? Simple, he had fired at a vicious dog earlier that day.

This explanation was not as ridiculous in 1901 as it sounds

253

today. In those days many cities were overrun with stray dogs. Everyone loved puppies, but apparently no one relished the expense of maintaining the fully grown animals.

With Sposato's trial for murder only a week away, Horace realized that he had no case at all. Public opinion in the Italian community was dead against his client. They only asked that a man they felt was a killer be punished. In desperation Horace placed an ad in the local newspaper requesting that anyone with information about the case come forward.

Horace received a phone call the first day of the advertisement. A lady's voice said simply, "I am Madame Lovell. You will find me at 1529 Glenarm Place." Within the hour Horace was knocking at the door. The door opened and Horace entered another world, complete with crystal ball, velvet drapes and, above all, the great English gypsy seer, Madame Lovell.

About sixty, Madame Lovell was a professional fortune teller, caster of spells and what have you. She was also blunt. She led off with a good line, near and dear to the heart of any self-respecting defence lawyer. "I can free your client," she said. Of course, there was a small matter of remuneration, but Horace set the Madame straight. Ethics forbad a lawyer from purchasing testimony. However, Horace let her know that if she cooperated he was not one to forget a favour, when and if she ever found herself in trouble. Speaking of trouble, there was one thing the Madame thought Horace should know from the outset. That was the embarrassing but undeniable fact that Madame Lovell had served time. Nothing big, mind you, just a minor misunderstanding over a customer's money many years before.

Enough chit chat. Madame deeply inhaled, and told Horace that she had a signed confession from John Brindisi revealing exactly what happened on the night of the murder. Amazingly enough, Madame produced the document. In it Brindisi revealed that he and his brother-in-law had lain in wait for Sposato and shot at him. Sposato had returned the fire in self-defence as he had always maintained. A confederate had picked up Lotito's gun and hidden it before police arrived on the scene. Horace was elated, but knew that he could never use an unwitnessed statement obtained by a fortune-telling ex-con.

Madame suggested that she set Brindisi up for the next day. Horace and other witnesses could be present. That's how lawyer Horace Hawkins and two law clerks, Pat Carney and James Sullivan, happened to be hiding behind red velvet drapes while Madame Lovell worked her magic on John Brindisi.

The scene was right out of fiction. Horace had to bite his lip to convince himself that he wasn't imagining the unbelievable setting. All three men had placed a small identifying mark on the paper Brindisi was to use.

Brindisi, a bundle of nerves, entered the dimly lit room. Madame was all decked out in her long robes. Brindisi wanted to know the result of Lotito's murder. Would Sposato be convicted? Madame told him the answer could only be revealed to him if he again wrote down the truth of what had already taken place. If he was honest to the last detail she would know. She would then burn the incriminating paper and give him the ashes. Again Brindisi wrote out the details exonerating Sposato. This time he revealed the motive. Brindisi accused Sposato of being unfair to friends of his in court while doing his job as court interpreter. Because of his biased interpretation he had to die.

Madame picked up the signed marked paper and in one motion palmed it. She substituted another paper and ignited it. All this was done so quickly that Horace, peeking through the drapes, almost flipped his biscuit, thinking Madame was actually burning evidence that could save his client. Madame gave Brindisi the phony ashes, told him anything he wanted to hear, and ushered him out of her home. She even charged him twenty dollars for the sitting.

Sposato stood trial for murder. Horace caused a sensation by allowing Brindisi to tell a pack of lies before springing the

255

signed document on him while he was testifying. Confused and afraid not to tell the truth now that the statement had been read in court, Brindisi confessed that his previous testimony was false. He was later charged with perjury. Another witness came foward who had seen Sposato shoot a mad dog on the day of Lotito's death. He even led police to the dog's grave.

The jury took only a little over an hour to return a not guilty verdict. Sposato walked out of court a free man.

Horace Hawkins continued to practice law in Denver. In fact he remained in the same office for fifty years and always maintained that the greatest thrill of his career was the day he went to see a fortune teller whose opening remark was, "I can free your client."